Sacred Ground

Reflections on Lakota Spirituality and the Gospel

by
Ron Zeilinger, M. Div.

Tipi Press
St. Joseph's Indian School
Chamberlain, South Dakota 57326

Published by Tipi Press, St. Joseph's Indian School, Chamberlain, SD 57326.

Tipi Press is an outreach of the Sacred Heart Fathers and Brothers of St. Joseph's Indian School, Chamberlain, SD.

Printed in the United States of America by Tipi Press Printing, St. Joseph's Indian School, Chamberlain, SD.

ISBN 1-877976-04-0

Contents

Introduction

My name is Ron Zeilinger. I live in Chamberlain, South Dakota, with my wife, Lisa, and my son, Matthew. I work at St. Joseph's Indian School as the director of religious education. I have worked at the school for several years and have come to know and care about many Lakota people during that time. I always say that "God gave me big ears" meaning that they are physically big, but also that God gave me the gift of listening to others in order to really hear them.

When I first came to South Dakota eight years ago, I encountered the Lakota/Dakota culture and I realized that there was much to admire about the language and customs. Over the years, I have continued to learn about their spirituality which regards even the earth as sacred and all things within creation as having relationship, even the smallest creature, like the ant. Here is an ancient wisdom which regards each day as holy, not just one day called "Sunday," and which sees spiritual power in rocks and stones. The more I become acquainted with this spiritual way, the more I felt like Moses before the burning bush in the desert. It was by means of a little tree that God manifested Himself to him and said: "Take off your shoes for you are standing on holy ground!" This deep and powerful spirituality is not to be trifled with nor is it to be dismissed as easily as it was by the early missionaries who failed to recognize its value and strength. We must show respect, for we are standing on **sacred ground.**

I have heard a lot about the painful memories and experiences of my Lakota friends, and it is sad to realize that some of this was caused by missionaries and other Christian people who intended to help the Lakota but in reality harmed them. In some cases, the harm can't be undone. Some of the culture and knowledge of the "old ways" have been lost forever. Often this has amounted to something that must in all honesty be called religious persecution. "It can't happen in America," we say, but it already did, and it happened to the Lakota/Dakota people within **our** lifetime.

As we shall see later on, the past **must** be healed, and the Gospel and the Lakota tradition **must** be reconciled — it is no option. As this book goes to print, this imperative seems all the more urgent as news of another young person's suicide reaches us from a local reservation community. Challenged by this and the cries for help from other young people, we need to ask ourselves some hard questions: In what ways has the church failed these youths who are the future of the church? How has the church aided or impeded the development of a healthy self-concept among young Native Americans? Is it acceptable to be ''Indian'' in the church, in the liturgy? How have the past missionary efforts of the church contributed to, rather than healed, the fractured and disintegrated conditions among Native American families and communities today? To what extent does reconciliation of the past mean restoration of cultural values, symbols and expressions within the Christian family called the Lakota church?

The longer I worked at St. Joseph's Indian School, the more I felt that I could do something in partnership with the Lakota children and staff to remedy the way in which the church had deprived the Lakota in the past, of their own culture. They had been discouraged from expressing it in the life of the church, the sacraments, and worship services. One day, after weeks of hesitation springing from fear of criticism, I was walking along and thinking about the Last Supper at which Jesus was telling the apostles: ''Do this in memory of me.'' He was telling them to remember what He was going to suffer on behalf of all people throughout history, and to remember this in all times and places — all cultures. Just then something made me look up to the sky and above me circling around were twelve eagles. I stood in amazement, and I knew then that I must not hesitate because of fear or criticism to welcome the Lakota culture into the religious instructions and worship services at our school.

What we have accomplished at St. Joseph's Indian School is local and our own in a sense, and should not be copied by others until they have worked out for themselves with all the people what it is they want to do. This has been our experiment and I hope it encourages others as they struggle toward their own ways of doing things in worship.

This small book represents my thinking since then, as well as some practical experiences in trying to carry out this effort. Cultural adaptation of the Gospel and liturgy is not an easy task and I have made these attempts with all humility. I am probably the most pitiful person around to attempt such a thing, because there are more skillful and knowledgeable people who could have done a much better job than I. Thanks to my big ears, however, I have been able to listen to others, especially the Lakota people around me, as I tried to carry out this task. I have made some mistakes out of ignorance, and for these I beg forgiveness of the Lakota people. I extend my hand in a gesture of goodwill toward them. I hope they will tolerate a fool for Christ's sake.

Christmas, 1986

Note: Sioux is the name which was given by white men to the various plains people who are of one stock but linguistically varied. The linguistic groupings according to the people's own designation are: Lakota, Dakota and Nakota. Generally, South Dakota is populated by the Lakota/Dakota people on whose behalf this book is written. Sometimes for convenience, I refer to only one grouping.

Wopila

I want to acknowledge my debt of thanks to the following people who, in their own unique ways, have helped me put this book together. Including their names does not mean necessarily that they agree with all the contents, however.

Sister Genevieve Cuny OSF: Whose sharing, reading of the rough draft and response encouraged me.

Fr. Stan Maudlin OSB: Vicar of Indian Affairs, Diocese of Sioux Falls, SD, whose reading also helped make this book a reality.

Deacon Victor Bull Bear: Who provided an example of how a Catholic Deacon lives in his own life both traditions.

Steve Charging Eagle: Who told me the legend of how the sacred pipe was brought to the Lakota people.

Tom Charging Eagle: Who corrected so many of my misconceptions about the Lakota tradition.

Reverend Clyde Estes: Who shared patiently with me his experience and knowledge of the Dakota and Christian traditions as an Episcopalian priest.

Leroy Hairy Shirt: Who shared candidly with me about his own Christian faith and Lakota beliefs.

Pete Catches (Petaga): Who impressed upon me the importance of always being loyal to the Truth.

Jesse Taken Alive: Who shared his insights on reconciling what has happened to the Lakota in the past with living in the present.

Pete Taken Alive: For his example in reconciling both traditions.

Father William Stolzman SJ: For his distinctions and clarifications.

Fr. John Hascall OFM Cap: For his inspiration and spiritual insight.

Deacon Harold Condon: For his emphasis on healing and the sacraments.

I had a vision. I saw
four chariots coming out
from between the mountains.
One was pulled by red horses,
the second by black horses,
the third by white horses,
and the fourth by dappled horses.
I asked: What do these mean?

"These are the four winds,
they have just come from
the presence of the Lord
of all the earth,"
said the messenger.

Zechariah 6: 5

Chapter 1

Culture and Identity

This book is an attempt at showing that it is possible for a people such as the Lakota/Dakota to maintain their culture — their music, language, customs and prayer forms — while living the Gospel of Jesus Christ. The Lakota not only may do this, but also have a **right,** because they are creatures of the one Father who is Spirit over and in all things, in the same way that all other people on the face of the earth are. In their lives and that of their parents and grandparents before them — a tradition stretching back to the "ancient ones" — God has spoken to them in ways they could understand. They, too, have a tradition in which God revealed something of Himself to them. The great Light has shone on them with its own unique ray of color, for they have the "good red way" which has also guided them. This tradition and revelation have been leading them continuously in a direction toward the full understanding of the Truth for which all nations are searching. For them, it can be considered as another Old Testament and it ought not to be discarded because it is part of their growth in the Spirit. Therefore, it is a treasure to be safeguarded, remembered and transmitted to the young people, among whom there is an urgent need for stability and roots, as they search for their identity or struggle with the lack of it.

God heard the prayers of those people who kept lonely vigils on hilltops, making their vision quests, or who prayed with heart-rending cries to Him during the sundances year after year: "Great Spirit, have pity on us!" He set them on a sacred path that led to Him and He listened to them as any good Father knows how to do.

> What father among you would hand his son a stone when
> he asked for bread? If you then know how to give your chil-

dren what is good, how much more will the heavenly Father give the Holy Spirit to those who ask him?

Luke 11: 11-13

When they asked Him for bread He did not hand them a stone as Jesus has said, but gave them spiritual food to strengthen them for their journey — the Spirit himself.

In the beginning before the world as we know it came to be, there was God, His Word and His Spirit. Then God spoke His Word and His Spirit moved over the chaos to create the world and the beings that live in it. This God who is "mystery" (Wakantanka) is "great beyond our knowledge" (Job 36: 26). Yet, He has provided constant evidence of Himself in creation, for those persons who are sincere and humble. One of the saints named Ephrem said that God imprinted upon nature, the symbols and figures which manifest Him, and that He did this as a preparation for revealing Jesus the Word who was to be born when the time had come. Therefore, the purpose of the created world and the universe which surrounds it is to prepare humanity for His coming among us.

God had his own way of revealing himself through His Son, opening up the mystery of His true identity and His name and He has done this gradually and various ways among the people of the earth, including the Lakota as well. The knowledge of His Son grew organically from their history of successes and failures as the Holy Spirit and the presence of the Word in creation helped each culture discover how God was present to them in their history and traditions. Their unique experience of culture, leaders, prophets, and spirituality as they passed through the sea of their own difficulties comprises their salvation history.

"You are a light to my path" prays the psalmist in Psalm 105, and it is the Spirit now who helps them perceive those ways in which the Word has been present all along as they made their way. They, too, are joined with the disciples in this search.

> . . .they were making their way. . .discussing as they
> went all that had happened. Jesus approached and began
> to walk along with them but they did not recognize him.
> He said to them: How slow you are to believe! He inter-
> preted for them every passage which referred to Him. . .
> with that their eyes were opened and they recognized Him.
> "Were not our hearts burning inside us as He talked to us
> along the way?"   Luke 24: 13-35

The Church, having learned its lesson after centuries of trial and er-
ror in bringing the Gospel to many different cultures, has urged its
members to respect the traditions of prayer and spirituality that
are found all over the earth — some of which are just as ancient as the
Jewish and Christian traditions. Indeed, the Native American traditions have been developing in some cases on this continent for over a
period of 10,000 years or more, for the earliest human remains found
on this soil have been dated at 48,000 years old.

Formerly, Pope Paul VI spoke to the bishops of Asia during one of
his visits to that part of the world, and his words could just as well
have been addressed to Native Americans:

> The propagation of the Christian message must in no way
> cancel out or lessen these cultural and spiritual values, which
> constitute a priceless heritage. The Church must make herself
> in her fullest expression native to your countries, your cul-
> tures, your races. . .Let the Church draw nourishment from
> the generous values of venerable religions and cultures.
> —L'Osservatore Romano, April 21, 1974

When white missionaries encountered the native people of the
Great Plains, they found a people who were already deeply spiritual
and who lived by moral codes of their own. Generally, the attitude of
the Christian missionaries toward this spirituality was one of suspicion

and opposition. Once a member of a tribe converted to Christianity, he or she was expected to reject everything about the "old ways."

The dilemma for the Indian person was this: in order to save his/her soul, he had to give up his soul — that is, he had to cease thinking and acting as an Indian. There are men and women alive today who remember being punished for speaking in their native language; who remember when the sundance was forbidden by law, and praying with the sacred pipe or participating in sweat-lodges or vision-quests was frowned upon by their religious instructors. "Church" meant the white man's church, his way of worshipping. The Indian ways of worshipping were now to become obsolete, perhaps even "from the devil."

But what is Christianity or the Gospel? Must it be clothed in the values, culture and economy of the white society? Is it possible that Jesus is not asking the Indian people to cease being Indian once they accept his way, which is **himself** after all? "I AM THE WAY," he said, but this "way" is not synonymous with the white man's civilization. A young Lakota woman expressed very well this desire to remain Indian while living as a committed Christian:

> I am a Christian woman. Maybe you should accept us the way we want to be, and not try to make us what you want us to be. White Americans have tried to change us for 150 years — maybe it's time to give up.
>
> We don't need you to make decisions on how we should live. We know what we want for ourselves and our communities. Myself, I don't want to be in the mainstream, because this will mean giving up my culture and our land. I am proud of our culture — and after all the torture and after all that was taken away, this pride and our culture was one thing that couldn't be taken away and destroyed.

Conversion to Christ and entering his church doesn't have to mean destroying Indian identity and spirituality. It ought to be a process of recognizing what is already there in the native tradition because of the Spirit of Jesus. It is an experience of the wealth of the Spirit, and the Lakota convert can rejoice in both his Lakota identity and his Christianity. One Lakota parent was able to deal with the so-called "problem" of being thoroughly Lakota and Christian in his own unique way. His daughter had come to him disturbed about the warnings of an otherwise well respected missionary of 40 years who had told her that those who were open to Indian spirituality were dealing with the devil and eternal damnation. The daughter was torn, because she had experienced Indian spirituality as something good and she also respected this missionary. Consequently, she approached her father with her dilemma. He did not have a ready answer, but prayed a long time for guidance which finally came to him. He told his daughter that Christian Lakota now believe in the Trinity: Father, Son and Spirit. Then he told her that the Lakota have **always** believed in and prayed to the Spirit in their own spirituality and therefore Lakota spirituality was all right. Both he and the daughter were satisfied with this answer which seemed to assure them that they didn't have to reject their traditional and unique ties with the mystery of the Sacred Trinity.

It is a struggle for Native Americans who are attempting to be faithful to the teachings of Christianity and the truth as they have known it in the Lakota tradition. There are no books to guide them and often there is conflicting advice from clergymen and women. Therefore, they must pray a great deal and develop their own wise answers as the father just mentioned has done. As one holy man has put it: "Truth is truth and no foolish man can change that. I have to live my life according to the truth, and when I come to die, I must answer for the way I lived." God is putting before the sincere Lakota/Dakota person a challenge and task: to remain true to the traditional spirituality and continue to follow Christ who said, "I am the way, the truth and the life."

They will rise on wings like eagles.

Isaiah 40:31

Parable of the Buffalo

"Once there was a buffalo grazing out on the prairie, eating its way across a field of tall grass. As it went, it ate the grass but left the sticks alone." What does this little story mean? It means that in the end, we must remember that no culture or tradition is perfect and has all the answers to life's problems and difficulties. The Lakota must accept some things from their heritage while rejecting what is no longer meaningful, just as the white people (wasicus) must understand that some aspects of their way of life are in conflict with the Gospel of Jesus.

One of the first areas of the Lakota tradition which needs to be reflected upon is the identity of Wakantanka — the Great Spirit. To begin with, so that we may form a basis for comparison, a brief outline is given here of the Judeo-Christian concept of **God.** Then we will investigate the Lakota concept of the Great Spirit in the past and present as far as that is possible. In doing so, we will come to understand to whom it is that the Lakota have prayed for so many centuries, for this is the basis of their own identity.

Jewish and Christian Concepts:

For both Jews and Christians, God is a **father,** although for the Jews this was not a trinitarian statement as it is for Christians. This fatherhood is intimately linked with the notion of **creator** since he is the father of all living things, that is, creatures. We are said to be "made in his image and likeness" although it is made clear that this likeness does not reside in our bodily characteristics, rather our spiritual ones — intellect and will. As creatures and children, we have a derived existence therefore.

God is conceived of as a being who is both personal and intimate to our hearts and yet above and beyond our world. He is the power within each of us, as the **ground** of our being, and he is "absent" from us, since he is **Spirit** and not present to us as we are to one another in a tangible way. God, as **absolute reality,** introduces the notion of sin as well, since there is a certain order that is intended by him. The most basic order consists in seeking our complete human satisfaction in him and not in created things. Since we are made in this image, we are made to seek him as our final goal: in God alone is my soul at rest.

When we do not orientate ourselves in the way that God has intended for our happiness, we experience the alienation from God and ourselves which "sin" causes. Therefore, a re-orientation or conversion is in order if we are to be integral again.

In this regard, a Jewish theme that carries a special emphasis in the Old Testament is the "fear of the Lord." The majesty and power of God are often times regarded as terrifying or at least worthy of great respect. As Moses learned on Sinai, no one could see God and live. Respect and distance, as well as utter humility were the only way to approach him. Once a year his otherwise unmentionable name was spoken in the holy of holies of the Jewish temple.

Jewish and Christian Differences:

The genius of Jesus was that He marched straight into the holy of holies and uttered an entirely different name: **Abba.** It was the name a child uttered to an intimate and loving father. In his preaching, there followed one story after another which dealt with his familiar and merciful concept of God. To be sure, Emmanuel — God is for and with us — was also a concept in the Old Testament and the New, but Jesus went far beyond the intention of his own tradition, thereby creating his own. In his person and his preaching, he proclaimed an intolerably familiar and extravagantly merciful Abba. The ultimate

Christian message is that divine mercy "became flesh" in the person of Jesus himself.

Christian Theology:

Whatever later theologians would say about God's other worldliness and infinity, the New Testament has it that God, moved by the suffering of his own creation, expressed himself in history and that this expression (logos) took flesh as a person, a human being — Jesus. From then on, for Christians, God was understood in **trinitarian** terms. God is Father, Son, and Spirit, yet remains **one.** Two thousand years of reflection and theological writings have not made this concept understandable, yet we ought to attempt a description, through analogy and metaphor, since as divine images we have an intellect, as Anselm reminded us.

Christian thinking and belief sees God as intimately bound up with his creation. He is no longer a spirit apart from humanity, rather he is intimate with matter. Historically and from all eternity a "wedding" of human and divine took place at the moment of Jesus' conception. This is the uniqueness of Christianity, that God is defined in a vastly different way than in any other religion: Love. Within the teaching about the resurrection of Jesus there is, of course, the idea that death means transformation for all of us, but there is also the idea that matter is forever made holy. Matter is understood as the field of expression for God, therefore the material world takes on a sacred character. God is the potter and the world is the clay.

By way of summary, we find in the Judeo-Christian tradition a God who is simple, perfect, good, limitless, unchangeable, eternal, one yet existing in all things. Each one of these characteristics could demand a work in themselves for proper explanation, and they do in a remarkable study by Thomas Aquinas. Through him we receive the terse but profound definition of God as "self subsistent being itself."

God is such that he has caused all else, but is himself caused by nothing else. In the final analysis, the concept of God is open-ended in mystery. Thomas Aquinas tells us that God's effects help to demonstrate that He exists, even though they cannot help us know Him completely for what He is.

—**Summa Theologiae** (Volume 2, Ia, 4.2)

Lakota Concepts and Traditions:

The non-Indian missionaries who initially encountered the Lakota speaking peoples heard them speak with many names about their beliefs in the divine: Wakantanka, Tunkashila, Taku Skan-Skan. They also observed them pray with their sacred pipe pointed consecutively to the Four Directions or Winds (North, South, East and West). Furthermore, they heard them speak of the symbol of the eagle with as much reverence as due to a divine manifestation. Therefore, they asked the question so important to their efforts at conversion: Do the Lakota believe in one God or many? Or if there are many in their system of belief, is there one who is above all the others who would be comparable to the God of the Old Testament? The question still arises sometimes in pastoral situations in working with the Lakota people, since the names of Wakantanka and Tunkashila are still in use, while Taku Skan-Skan is also not forgotten. Our task here is to determine what is meant by these names, both in the past and in the present, as far as that is possible. Once this is determined, then we may compare them to the Judeo-Christian concepts of God to discover how they are alike and not alike.

Let us turn to some statements made by Lakota people, for who knows the tradition better than they? Let us begin with some historic figures who have died since but whose words remain.

Most Indians believe in the Great Spirit (Wakantanka), in a heaven and a hell, but some are unbelievers, and think that when they die they are no more, just like the dog and the horse. There are but two worlds, the one in which we live and the one where the Great Spirit dwells. All good men, whether white or red, go to heaven.   **—Spotted Tail**

In this passage, we find that Wakantanka is translated as the Great Spirit and practically speaking, it appears that this Great Spirit is at least the main concern within the Lakota belief system. The reference to "good men" implies that this Great Spirit is **good** as well, and where he is, is **heaven.** It is also apparent that there was no uniformity of belief at least in any kind of unanimous fashion among the Lakota. It is characteristic of the Lakota to be unconcerned with coercion or dogmatic definitions among traditionally religious circles.

Another famous person, one who eventually converted to Christianity (unlike Spotted Tail) was Chief Gall whose words we quote here. The occasion for these words was a conference that he called between himself and a preacher he had heard for a long time in the church near his home on the reservation. Again, we are given access to the spiritual mind of a man who was not brought up in the Christian mentality. Once again, the reader is referred to the passage quoted previously:

What is entirely new to me is that the Wakan is actually the Father of all men and so loves even me and wants me to be safe. This man you talk about has made Wakantanka very plain to me whom I only groped for once, in fear. Whereas I once looked about me on a mere level with my eyes and saw only my fellow man to do him good, now I know how to look up and see God my Father, too. It is waste (good).

—Chief Gall

Chief Gall speaks out of the experience of the Wakan as fearful — a notion that is akin to the Old Testament fear of the Lord. The symbol of the live, exposed electric wire has been used to express something of the distance and respect that is experienced in the presence of the divine. The Indian mentality would readily identify with the God whom Moses experienced, with images of mountain, thunder and lightning. The Wakan was nothing to be "fooled with," and any wrong or irresponsible actions might court disaster for the individual and community.

Another traditional man who had something to say about this matter was Black Elk who is particularly knowledgeable in both traditions since he was akin to a "medicine man" in his earlier days, and then became an active and dedicated catechist in the Catholic religion later. Black Elk speaks intimately of his prayer experiences:

> Now I light the pipe and after I have offered it to the powers that are one Power, and sent forth a voice to them, we shall smoke together.
> Grandfather, Great Spirit, you have always been and before you no one has been. There is no other one to pray to but you. You yourself, everything that you see, has been made by you.   **—Black Elk**

This prayer is typical of the prayers that are attributed to Black Elk. He intertwines many themes and we shall attempt to unravel each of them for investigation. The "powers" that are "one Power" probably refer to the four directions, the earth and the sky, since apparently he is involved in praying with the sacred pipe. At least in his mind, all of these powers (or spirits as some would say) coalesce into one. The difficulty here as elsewhere in these texts and references is **language** — since some words and concepts are not translatable or difficult to parallel in another language. Often in her classic work on **Teton Sioux Music,** Frances Densmore refers to this difficulty:

In the mind of the Sioux the meaning of the word **wakan** contains more of mystery and a greater element of the supernatural than we are accustomed to associate with the words "sacred" or "holy," though these are used as its English equivalent. (p. 121)

After Black Elk says that "everything has been made" by this Great Spirit, he goes on to list them: the four directions or winds, the thunder beings, the earth, the heavens and the eagle. Each of these so-called spirits or objects of spiritual address are creatures of the one Great Spirit after all.

"Grandfather" is a translation of **Tunkashila** and is used by Black Elk interchangeably with **Wakantanka.** This name connotes One who is so ancient as to preclude anyone or thing older than he. Oral tradition has it that one may find nothing older than the rocks on this earth and thus there is a root connection between Tunkashila and **tunkan** (sacred stone). The phrase, "you have always been" consequently is a further development of this name. The phrase, "before you no one has been" certainly gives primacy to this Great Spirit over all other spirits and created things. Finally, the phrase, "there is no other to pray to but you" is decisive, in that Black Elk places this Great Spirit, Wakantanka as the One ultimately worthy of prayer. Black Elk also makes a statement elsewhere about the **four directions** which indicates that although they are addressed in prayer and honored with the pipe, they are not divine in their own right, but seem to be manifestations of the Great Spirit.

> . . .but these four spirits (four directions) are only one
> Spirit after all, and this eagle feather here is for that One.
> **—Black Elk**

The compilation of oral myths by James Walker entitled **Lakota Myth,** has a passage in which Sky is addressing Earth, Rock and Sun and tells them that they are all from one and the same source, namely Wakantanka. Sky goes on to say that no one can understand him, not even they:

Because each of them is only a part of Wakantanka and he is the God of all other spirits and powers.

As anyone who has studied the phenomenon of myths knows, they are not philosophical or historical statements, but they do present truth in a way that must be taken seriously. Therefore the kernel of truth which we are able to glean from this passage seems to be that Wakantanka is unsurpassed and the source all other powers and beings. This passage also informs us rather clearly of the meaning of Wakantanka in the words of Sky: no one can understand him, he is the Great Mystery. This is by far a more accurate translation of the name Wakantanka, for as we saw, "wakan" denotes a mystery that is awe-inspiring, while the word "tanka" means something great. This divine mystery is so great as to be beyond all understanding, even the understanding of spiritual beings and powers who operate on a plain above mankind but below Wakantanka.

I would like to conclude this section with a quote from a man who was contemporary with our own times and who exercised a great amount of authority among the Lakota as a "holy man." He assists our understanding of the Lakota mentality in these words:

You can't explain it except by going back to the circles within circles idea, the spirit splitting itself up into stones, trees, tiny insects even, making them all **wakan** by his ever-presence. And in turn all these myriad of things which makes up the universe flowing back to their source, united in the one Grandfather Spirit.   **(Lame Deer)**

One cannot speak of dogma as existing among the Lakota, since, according to their attitude, every man is free to believe in his own way without pressure from any higher authorities. Lame Deer, however, functioned for years as a medicine man and ritual leader and may be considered somewhat of an expert on tradition. He was highly respected as one who knew and understood a spirituality that is considered by many to be older than the Bible.

If we keep in mind the characteristics of the Judeo-Christian God, at least as **Father,** we will see remarkable similarities with the Lakota concept of Wakantanka or Tunkashila. He seems to be **one,** the **source of all things** whether the physical world or the spiritual realities, **present everywhere** in this creation by giving each creature a share in his life by the degrees in which they are intended. He is considered to be **prior** to anything else and **not dependent on anything else for his being,** in fact, he **always existed.** He alone is worthy of and is the sole object of **prayer** in the strict sense. To be sure the other spirits and powers addressed are considered as worthy of reverence, (not unlike the ''saints and angels'' who are honored in the liturgy) but they are never given the primacy of place that is reserved to the One Great Spirit, Wakantanka.

The concept of Wakantanka is left in the realms of the incomprehensible, for the sacred myth concludes as Thomas Aquinas does, that he is ultimately a mystery beyond the capabilities of all human understanding.

There is no equivalent in Lakota history to the appearance of Jesus in the history of mankind as a divine savior. It never occurred to them that a man might receive such honor from God as to be raised up to the status of Wakantanka. There is a feeling for the holiness of the material world, but this is not derived from its being made holy because of an incarnation by God. The conversion statements by some of the people we have quoted also attest to the fact that this Great Spirit was not defined as ''love,'' although he could be approached in prayer, and aid and wisdom might be forthcoming. He was always approached with the greatest respect and humility. Such power is helpful, but also potentially dangerous.

I'm telling you what I myself know. . .what I tell you is what I learned from Dreamer of the Sun, who taught me as he was taught. . .He thus decided to instruct me and began my training at an early age. One of the first and most important things I was taught was that I must have the greatest reverence for Wakantanka.

Red Weasel

He pitched his tent among us.   John 1, 10

Chapter 2

The Lakota Tradition

The life of the Lakota people has been and still is very bound to tradition (Lakol Wicohan). One hears of doing things as a "traditional" Indian, or of doing it the "Indian way," but what exactly is meant by this? There are a great many things that come under the category of the traditional Indian way of living. There are objects such as sweet grass and tobacco and belief in spirits, Wakantanka and the Four Directions or Winds. The following summary is a brief look at the tradition which is woven into the very fabric of the Lakota life. These things are so much a part of their life that if they were forcibly removed or forbidden, as they have been at times in the past, one would wonder if the people could survive for very long. The people are still recovering from the effects of religious persecution which they endured during the beginning of this century at the hands of the United States government and the various churches. With great respect, let us view the Lakota tradition.

The White Buffalo Woman and the Pipe

Long ago, the Lakota were camping. Two young men left the camp and were hunting, when suddenly a very beautiful woman appeared. She was climbing a hill and coming toward them. She was carrying a bundle in her arms. One of the men began thinking unclean thoughts about her and said that he was going to her. But the other man said they ought to be careful because she is not just an ordinary woman but something holy — **wakan.**

But the other man was not convinced by this and started out walking towards the woman. As he came close to her, a cloud covered him and when it went away he was lying on the ground dead. Seeing this, the other young man stood there shaking.

The beautiful woman said that he was not to feel afraid because she was bringing something to the people that will help them live. She asked him to go and tell the people that she would be coming to them soon.

After that, the young man hurried back to the camp and told the herald to announce to everyone that something was about to happen and that they should get ready for it.

So all the people got themselves ready by keeping good thoughts in their minds and by behaving in a good way.

Finally, one day the woman came walking toward the camp singing. She came walking among their tipis and when she stopped, she told the people that she had something for them.

It is said that she was very beautiful and that she was dressed in white buckskin, with very long hair. She opened her bundle and showed the sacred pipe to the people. Twelve eagle feathers hung from the pipe. She handed the pipe to the leader of the people and told him that this was the sacred pipe and that the Great Spirit will bless them with good because of it.

The woman then showed the people how to pray with the pipe, lifting it up to the sky, lowering it to the earth, and pointing it in the four directions.

The woman addressed the women, telling them that it was the work of their hands and the fruit of their wombs that kept the people alive.

Then she turned to the little children and said that they should be treated with the same respect as the adults. She told the little children that what grown men and women did was done for them. She told them that children were the greatest possession of the nation, they are the coming generations, the life of the people and the circle without end.

Then she spoke to the men like a sister. She made them understand that everything that they depended upon came from the four direc-

The Great Spirit will bless you with good because of this.

tions, the earth and the sky. They should use the pipe to offer prayers to Wakantanka for everything that he gives them in life. They should pray with it every day. They should be kind to the women and children and love them.

Last of all, she spoke to the leader. It was his duty to take care of the pipe. She told him that it should be used when the people are threatened by war or sickness, or any great need. She told him that eventually, she would reveal to them seven sacred rites in the future.

It is said that she stayed with them four days and continued to teach them how to live good lives and about the pipe and its meaning.

When she was finished, she sang a song and went away from the camp. As the people watched her go away, she suddenly turned into a white buffalo. It snorted, ran away and went out of sight.

It may be that from this time on the people began to use the prayer "Mitakuye Oyasin" or "All My Relatives," since it was the White Buffalo Woman who taught them with these words.

Throwing the Ball

Before this rite — which is a game — takes place, a special tipi is put up and the floor covered with sage. Before sunrise, a holy man goes in and sits down at the West and clears a place in the dirt for some hot coals. When the coals are ready, he burns sweet grass on them and blesses or "purifies" the pipe, the buffalo skull, the ball and everything else that is going to be used in this rite. He purifies them by passing them through the smoke of the sweet grass.

When the sun is beginning to come up and the light enters the tipi, the holy man makes an altar out of a mound of dirt. He also draws lines to the four directions and sprinkles tobacco on them. In this way, the altar is like the whole universe.

Then the girl who is chosen to throw the ball that day is brought in

Happy the one who finds wisdom.   **Proverbs 3:13**

and she sits down at the left side of the holy man. Next the holy man picks up the ball that he has made from buffalo hide and stuffed with buffalo hair. He paints it red and then paints two blue circles around the ball, crossing them over each other. (The color red stands for the earth, and the color blue stands for the sky.) The two circles join the four directions together. In this way, he makes the ball sacred because it brings the earth and the heavens together.

Then the holy man prays with the pipe, pointing the stem up to the sky and asking the Great Spirit to look upon them as they hold the pipe in one hand and their children in the other. After that, he gives the ball to the girl by placing it in her left hand, and tells her to lift her right hand up to the sky toward the Great Spirit. He holds the pipe in his left hand and raises his right hand up to the sky also.

He prays about how the ball represents the universe and calls upon the Four Directions and the heavens to witness what they are doing. He thanks the Great Spirit for being with them as they perform these sacred actions.

Next the holy man paints the buffalo skull which has been present there, but before he does this, he prays in thanksgiving for all that was given to them through the buffalo's help — food, clothing, and shelter. It is because of these things that they are alive and well. Then he paints a red line around the head and down between the horns. After he has done this, he explains how this rite came about in a vision about the buffalo.

He says that the mother buffalo had a newborn calf and helped it get up and walk by snorting and nudging at it. She encouraged it until it was able to get up and stand on its own strength. In this way, the mother passed on the knowledge of how to get along in life, to grow up and live well on one's own as an adult. Sometimes it was a struggle but the task was to keep trying until the goal was grasped.

Then the holy man explains that he is giving the ball to her and that she is going to throw the ball to the people, because the ball represents the wisdom of how to get up and live well. The round ball stands for the world and living creatures on it, as well as Wakantanka himself since the whole world is his home. Whoever struggles and catches this ball receives a great blessing.

After these words, the holy man and the girl leave the tipi and walk to the place where the ball is to be thrown. Once there, the girl faces the West and then throws the ball to the people. She does this in each of the Directions and each time someone catches the ball and then brings it back to her where she is standing at the center of the game circle. The last time she throws the ball straight up into the air and when it is caught, it is given back to her for the last time.

After this sacred game is over, the holy man prays with the pipe and asks the Great Spirit to watch over all the people that He has placed on this earth. It is from this Spirit that all wisdom has come, who teaches us how to walk in wisdom with all things as their relatives. Then the pipe is touched by all who are gathered around for the ball throwing ceremony. The ones who catch the holy ball are then given presents and there is a big feast to which everyone is invited.

Today, this rite does not seem to be in practice anymore, but more and more, many of the old ways are being restored to the people. Perhaps this rite, too, will be reinstated one day for the benefit of the people.

Crying for a Vision

This ritual has never been abandoned by the people and is still in use today.

There are different reasons why people want to make a vision quest:

1) to understand a vision better that they have already received.
2) to prepare themselves for the Sundance.
3) to ask for a favor from Wakantanka.
4) to thank Wakantanka for a special gift He has given them.

**Your young men shall see visions
and your old men shall dream dreams.**
Joel 3: 1-5

5) to realize that we are close to all things and especially to the Great Spirit.

When someone wants to make a vision quest, he takes a pipe and brings it to a holy man, and asks him for his help. If the holy man agrees to help him, a day is set aside for a sweatlodge.

On that day, the holy man and some helpers go into the sweatlodge with the one who is going to make the vision quest. All the things he is going to use on the quest are purified — his pipe, buffalo robe and offering sticks. Then they are set outside and the sweatlodge is done in the usual way.

When all of that is finished, everyone leaves the sweatlodge and the vision seeker takes all his things with him and goes to the bottom of a high hill. He stays there until the holy man and his helpers have prepared everything at the top.

On top of the hill a place is cleared and a pole is put at the center of this place with some tobacco offerings tied to it. Other small poles are set up in the four directions, with offerings tied to each of them, too. Also, sage is put around the center of the clearing so that the vision seeker can lie down near the center pole and rest when he is tired. When everything is ready, the holy man and his helpers go down to the bottom of the hill to the vision seeker.

Now the vision seeker climbs alone with his pipe, buffalo robe and offering sticks to the top of the hill, praying all the time he is climbing:

Great Spirit have pity on me,
that my people may live!

When he gets to the spot that has been cleared for him, he goes to the center pole and faces West. Then he walks out from there to the pole that is in the West. There he begins praying with the pipe in his hands. Then he returns to the center pole and goes from there to the North. In the same way, he prays to the other two directions as well as to the sky and to the earth.

This is how he prays while he is on the hill and he can take as much time as he wants in any direction. When he finishes going around once, he starts all over again, all day long and into the night. When he gets tired, he may sleep on the sage with his head next to the center pole. All the time that he is on the hill, he does not eat or drink. He will feel very weak and tired when night comes.

Some people spend one day and one night seeking a vision, and others spend two, three or even four days. Usually they do not spend more than four days and nights.

If the vision seeker prays from the heart and pays attention, some messages will come to him. They may come through nature in a bird or animal. Sometimes even ants have given messages if the seeker is listening and looking. After all, the Great Spirit can use anything to speak to us and he often does.

When the time is up, the holy man and his helpers come up to get the seeker and take him down to a sweatlodge. During the sweatlodge, the seeker tells them what he heard and saw while he was praying on the hill alone. He tells them everything, being careful not to make anything up. When he is finished, the holy man prays to Wakantanka, the Great Spirit, thanking Him for all that He has given, especially for having had pity on this person who was seeking help from Him.

Becoming A Woman

When a young girl becomes a grown woman, something sacred happens to her. Now she can have children and she has to be made ready for all her responsibilities with a special ceremony.

In preparing for this ceremony, a sacred tipi is put up and then the holy man comes and purifies the pipe and everything that will be used in the ceremony. Only the close relatives and the girl are allowed into this tipi. Then he prays for help in making this girl ready to become a woman, so that she will be purified and made sacred. He prays also for all the children that will enter the world because of her.

Your wife will be like a fruitful vine.   Psalm 128: 3

He calls on the Four Directions, the earth and sky, the animals and birds — all living creatures, as well as the Great Spirit Wakantanka above all to join in helping them. When he has finished praying with the pipe, everyone leaves except the family of the girl, and he sings a song about preparing a sacred place. When he has finished this song, he goes around the tipi breathing like a buffalo — on the girl, the altar made of earth, and everything else in the tipi. Then he digs a small hole in the middle of the tipi that looks like a buffalo wallow. He puts the dirt from this into a pile and puts the buffalo skull on it, facing East. In front of this skull, he puts a bowl of water which has some choke cherries in it.

Next, he makes a bundle of sweet grass, cherry tree bark and some hair from a live buffalo. He holds this bundle over the girl's head and prays for her to the Great Spirit, asking Him to bless her and make her fruitful with children. Then, as he prays toward each direction, he passes the bundle down the side of her that is facing that direction which he is addressing at the time. He prays that the waters of the West will make her clean, that she will receive purity from the North, wisdom from the East, and a blessing from the South from whence many people have come and gone.

Then he picks up the buffalo skull and begins to push her towards the bowl of water. She kneels down and drinks four sips from the bowl. Next he takes a piece of buffalo meat which has been prepared and offers it to the Four Directions as well as the sky and the earth. Then he holds it in front of the girl and tells her to go among the people as an example to them. She is to be humble and kind to others. She must never forget how God cares for her, and in turn must take care of others, especially the little children.

Then he places the meat in the girl's mouth and passes the bowl of water for all to drink. He picks up the pipe after this has been done and prays to Wakantanka on behalf of the girl, her family and relatives and all children who are going to be born.

Then the girl is brought out of the sacred tipi and all the people come up and put their hands on her to bless her and wish her well.

Everyone has a feast after that and there is a give-away. The poor receive many good things on that day.

This rite does not seem to be practiced anymore, but perhaps it, too, will be revived one day.

The Sweatlodge

The sweatlodge itself is made from twelve to sixteen willow poles. These poles are bent over each other and stuck into the ground, and covered with hides or blankets. When it is finished, it stands for the universe. Usually, the door faces the West where the rain comes from in the clouds and storms.

The round fireplace at the center of the sweatlodge stands for the center of the universe, where Wakantanka lives. In it are put the rocks that were heated in a fire outside and brought in with forks. Sage covers the floor all around. A path leads out of the door to a small dirt mound which is the altar where the sacred pipe is kept.

When it is time to start the ceremony, those who are going to take part in it come in through the door and say a prayer to Wakantanka who has put them on this earth, to purify them and help them in what they are doing. In this and in all things, they need His help as humble creatures.

Once they are inside, the people sit in a circle on the sage. Everyone is silent and then the pipe is passed in and everyone watches as the hot rocks are brought in and put in the pit. When the pit is filled, the leader offers the pipe to the four directions, heaven and earth. Then he lights it, smokes it and passes it around to everyone. When they have all smoked the pipe, it is put outside on the altar with the stem facing the West. When the pipe is brought out each time, it will have its stem in one of the other directions until the sweatlodge is finished.

Then the flap is pulled over the door and the sweatlodge becomes completely dark. The leader pours some water on the rocks and the

I will pour clean water over you and you will be cleansed. . . I will remove your hearts of stone and give you hearts of flesh instead.   Ezekiel 36: 26

steam fills the whole inside. Praying to the West, he asks the Great Spirit to look on him and all the people and help them with what they need, so that they may live.

After a while, the flap is opened and water is passed around for everyone to drink. Then the pipe is brought in and smoked by everyone in the circle. Then, when the pipe is put outside again, the flap is closed and the same thing goes on again. It happens in this way until the leader has prayed to all four directions.

Each of the directions have their special meaning:

West: This is where thunder and rainstorms come from and all creatures owe their lives to this water.

North: This is where the powerful winds come from that cleanse us and make us pure as snow.

East: This is where the Morning Star is seen before dawn and where the sun comes up. It helps us see things wisely.

South: This is where life comes from and when people die it is said that their souls return in this direction — "gone south."

When prayers have been said by the leader to the last direction, he talks to everyone about how Wakantanka has blessed them and how dependent they are on Him for everything. He is their light in the darkness so that they can see things correctly with the heart.

Then the flap of the sweatlodge is opened and everyone comes out and prays to Wakantanka in a spirit of thankfulness. As they leave the sweatlodge, each one says: "All my relatives!"

It is important to know that this rite of the sweatlodge helps those who take part in it as well as all people. It is done when someone wants to purify themselves in order to prepare for God's help and blessings, either for himself personally or for others.

This ritual is still in use among the people, both before and after other rites such as the vision quest and sundance. Sweatlodges are often located near their homes so that the people can make frequent use of them both in summer and winter.

Making Relatives

On the day of the ceremony, the people should get up before the sun comes up and get themselves ready. While they are doing this, the holy man paints his body red and puts on a headdress with buffalo horns. Then he goes to the top of a nearby hill and faces the sun as it comes up. He sings a song of praise and asks for a blessing on all the people.

A small tipi is put up which will be used for all the preparations, and a large tipi which will be used for the ceremony. When they are done, the holy man's helpers go into the large tipi to make an altar and spread sage on the floor. They dig a hole in the center of the tipi for a fireplace. They also put a buffalo skull and a stone beside the altar. The stone stands for God, who is the Grandfather of all things. Finally, they set up a scaffold on the south side of the tipi where the Hunka meat will be placed.

When they are done with all these things, the holy man comes with everything he will use for the ceremony: horse tail wands, Hunka corn stick, rattles and a fire carrying stick. He gives these to his helpers and then sings a song to the four directions. They all march behind him in a circle outside the large tipi. As they are marching, the one who will become "Hunka" goes into the small tipi and waits for the holy man to come. When the holy man stops singing outside the small tipi, he says to the people that there is an "enemy" inside and asks who will accompany him as he enters to capture him. Then he shouts that those who are "hunka" should be ready to die for each other, and with those who have joined him, he rushes inside and captures the one who will become a hunka that day.

He takes him over to the large tipi singing a victory song as they go. At the doorway, he says to everyone that they should "kill" this enemy, unless someone is willing to take him for a hunka. Then the one who will sponsor him steps forward and agrees to take him for one. After this happens, the holy man agrees to make him one and everyone enters the large tipi and sits down. Those who cannot sit in-

He gave up His life for us and we, too, ought to give up our lives for our brothers. **I John 3:16**

side, sit in a circle outside the doorway. Last of all, the holy man enters and sits in the place of honor, facing the altar and the one who will be made a hunka and his sponsor.

He fills the pipe, lights it and gives it to the one who is to become a hunka first. Then the sponsor receives it and finally it is passed around for everyone to smoke. The last one to smoke it is the holy man and then he asks the Great Spirit to look down on everyone present and bless them in what they are about to do as well as during their lives afterward.

The helpers put some special hunka ceremonial meat on the scaffold and when they are finished, he looks toward the buffalo skull and addresses it. He says that this meat was once the buffalo's and now it has provided them with this food.

Then he gives some sweet grass to the helper who puts it on the fire. Its good smell fills the whole tipi and the holy man prays. He asks that no evil will come near them in this place while they perform these ceremonies and that God bless them.

After this, he says to the one who will become hunka that he is going to teach him how to behave like a true relative and that the other hunkas will teach him, too, if he is willing to listen to them and their good advice. Then each of them talk to the one who is to become a hunka and tell him what it means to be a hunka and how he must act if he wishes to be one.

After this, the helpers stand up with the hunka wands made of long flowing horse hair and wave them over the one who is becoming a hunka. While they are doing this, the holy man prays that he be shielded from harm and receive the power to do good. Then he himself takes a wand in each hand and waves them from side to side over the one becoming a hunka and then he turns and waves them over all the hunkas present as well. He sings a song as he does this and all the people join in.

After this, he takes a rattle in each hand and rattles them over the head of the one becoming a hunka and also over all the hunkas who are there. He prays that the sound of these rattles will call down God's attention on everyone present at this ceremony.

He takes the hunka corn stick and pushes the stem into the dirt altar and explains that their Mother Earth has given this corn and that in this way she teaches them to give food to the hungry in the same way. Then he removes the corn stick from the dirt and gives it back to the helper.

Next he takes the special meat from the scaffold and gives it to the one who is becoming a hunka. He tells him to give some of it to everyone in the tipi but the holy man does not take any for himself. While everyone is sitting and eating this meat, the holy man says to the one becoming hunka that even if he has some food in his mouth and sees someone who is hungry, he ought to take it out of his own mouth and give it to that hungry person.

Then he says that he ought to take his moccasins from his own feet and give them to another when he sees someone who has none or they are old and worn.

If he sees someone who is cold and has nothing to wear, then he ought to take off his own clothes and give them to that person. He should strip himself and give everything he has to another person who is poor.

Next the holy man tells the sponsor and the one becoming a hunka to sit side by side. The helper holds a robe over them so that no one else can see them. Then the holy man ties them together, arm to arm and leg to leg. After this, the robe is taken off and he explains to the one becoming a hunka that they have been bound to each other, and that what each one has now belongs to the other. Now they must help each other in every way and that what is done to one is the same as being done to the other.

Then the holy man stands up and declares that this one is now a hunka. The ceremony is over then, and the new hunka along with his sponsor leave for the small tipi where they untie themselves. After that, they get dressed and join the rest of the people. Gifts are given away by the new hunka and his relatives, and there is a feast to which everyone is invited.

This rite exists today in a modified form.

Keeping of the Soul

When a child dies and the parents want to do something special and sacred about it, they call for a holy man who shows them how to "keep" the soul of their child with them for awhile.

A special tipi is set up where the soul will be kept for one year. Then one of the first things the holy man does is to pray to Wakan-tanka and then cut a little hair from the child's head. Then he blesses it over some smoke from burning sweet grass and wraps it up in some buckskin. After that, it is hung up in the special tipi.

Then the holy man lights the sacred pipe, prays with it, and passes it around to all the people who have gathered inside the tipi. After this, the body of the child is taken out and buried. He tells the parents how they should live from now on, because their child's soul is being kept there in this tipi. They should not fight or argue, and always keep the soul of their child in mind. No bad person should be allowed to enter the tipi. Whenever the parents eat, they should leave something for the soul of the child. If anyone wants to leave gifts, they should keep these gifts in a special box, and give them away to the poor and the needy later.

After one year has gone by, the holy man comes back again. This time he is going to release the soul. Another special tipi is put up and when the holy man is sitting down in it, the mother goes to the tipi where the soul is being kept and brings back the sacred bundle with the lock of hair in it. Then the holy man speaks to the soul in the bundle, telling it that this is a day on which the Great Spirit is it and everyone present, therefore this is a sacred day for God is with them in a special way.

Then the holy man prays to Wakantanka with the pipe. He asks him to look with mercy on the people there and the soul that is going to be released. The pipe is smoked by everyone who is there and then some buffalo meat and cherry juice are brought in. Some of it is put before the sacred bundle and the rest of it is given to four girls to eat. They have been chosen to do this and they are virgins. These girls are reminded that from now on they should share what they have with those who are poor.

Then the holy man picks up the sacred bundle and says that this soul is going to leave them on a sacred journey.

Before the holy man goes out of the tipi with the sacred bundle, the father embraces it and the holy man assures the father that if he is good to all the people who are still alive, then the memory of this beloved child will live on.

As the holy man walks through the door of the tipi with the sacred bundle, he calls on the soul of the deceased to remember those people that are left behind as it leaves on its sacred journey and to help them stay on the sacred path as well.

At this moment, the soul is released and makes its way to Wakantanka along the "spirit path."

After that, the family and relatives celebrate by sharing a meal and giving gifts away.

This rite does not seem to exist intact, but attitudes about the dead still remain and it is very important for the family and relatives to remember the deceased on the anniversary of their death with a feast and a give-away.

Sundance

When the Lakota want to do something really special for the people, they make the promise to take part in the Sundance. The Sundance is a sacred ritual in which the dancer offers himself — his body

Death is the destiny of every man.　　　　**Ecclesiastes 7: 2**

— on behalf of the people. His crying and pleading to the Great Spirit while dancing around the cottonwood tree bring blessing and power to their lives. He is willing to suffer any kind of pain if it means that the circle of life will be made strong and the people will live good lives.

First a holy man is sent by himself to find a cottonwood tree that is the right size and shape. It will stand in the middle of the dancing circle. When he finds the tree, he returns to tell the people and they come back with him, singing. When they are standing around the tree, some women who are going to have babies dance around it. They do this because the Spirit of the Sun loves everything that bears fruit.

After they have finished dancing, a warrior strikes the tree, counting "coup" on it. Since he has done this, he has to give away gifts to the most needy people. The braver he is, the more he gives away.

Then some young girls come to the tree carrying axes and singing. These girls have to be virgins and they must be so good that no one can criticize them. They are the ones who chop the tree down and trim the branches off.

When the girls have finished their work, the leaders of the people carry the tree home. On the way, they stop four times, once for each season of the year. Each time they stop, they give thanks for a season.

Before the tree arrives at the camp, some of the young men make a contest. They act like warriors and race to the spot where the tree will stand. Whoever touches the sacred spot first will not be killed in war that year.

Then the tree is placed in the center of the dancing circle, and it is put into place by holy men who sing sacred songs and make vows to the Spirit.

The following day, the dancers fast and go into the sweatlodge to purify themselves. They pray to be made ready for dancing. When they come out, they dress for the dance. They wear sage wreaths on their heads with eagle feathers on them. They also wrap beautiful blankets around their waists and have eagle bone whistles hanging around their necks.

As the dancers stand at the West looking up at the tree, they hold their hands raised. The leader says a prayer to Wakantanka, the Great Spirit to look down on the dancers and the sacred tree. He prays that their prayers and suffering will bring good to the people and that He will take pity on them as they are gathered here and always.

Throughout the sacred days while the singers are singing and drumming, all the dancers move around the circle raising their hands to the tree and blowing on their eagle bone whistles. Finally, each one of them goes to the center and lies down beneath the tree, where they are pierced.

Piercing means that an eagle claw or sharp stick is pushed through the skin on the chest, and a long leather string is tied from the tree to the claw or stick. After this is done, each of the dancers gets up and starts dancing around the tree. While they are moving around the tree in a wide circle, they blow on their eagle bone whistles and pull back. They do this so that after a while they can tear themselves loose from the tree. Some dancers take a long time to do this, others do not.

When they tear loose, they return to the tree and lie down while the leader puts healing plants on their wounds. Then they rest for awhile until it is time for them to rejoin the group.

When everyone has finished dancing, the leader takes the sacred pipe and prays to the Great Spirit asking Him to hear the voices that have been raised to Him in their suffering. He tells Wakantanka that they wish to live and grow, as relatives with all created things.

When he finishes, everyone smokes the pipe and then the dancers leave for the sweatlodge. There the leader talks to them about the sacred things they have done during this sundance and how they ought to have pity on others from now on. By giving of their bodies and souls to Wakantanka, they have made the people stronger.

After the sweatlodge is finished, all the dancers join the rest of the people for a feast. Everyone is happy because the Sundance has made the lives of the people strong again. Many gifts are given to the dancers and they are honored.

It is a credit to the Lakota people who have maintained this

He bore in his own body our sins on the tree and by his wounds you have been healed. 1 Peter 2:24

"From the four winds come, O Spirit!"   **Ezekiel 37:1**

beautiful and moving ritual despite many years of attempted suppression by church and government.

The Four Directions

When the Lakota people pray or do anything sacred, they see the world as having four directions. From these four directions come the four winds, and each direction has a special meaning and color that belongs to it. The cross symbolizes all of them.

East (Yellow): This is the direction from which the Sun comes. Light dawns in the morning and spreads over the whole. It is the beginning of the day and the beginning of understanding because light helps us see things the way they really are. Darkness goes away. The deeper meaning is that the East stands for the wisdom that helps people live good lives. This is why traditional people get up in the morning to pray facing the dawn, asking God for wisdom and understanding.

This is the kind of prayer that can be said toward the East:

As I hold the Sacred Pipe in prayer
for you to see and hear,
lead us Great Spirit, by the light
of your wisdom.
Thank you Great Spirit for all the ways
in which you guide us.
We are lost without you.

South (White): This direction stands for warmth and growing things, because when the sun is in the south, it is highest in the sky. Its rays are powerful in drawing life from the earth.

That is why it is said the life of things comes from the south. Also warm and pleasant winds blow from this direction. It is said in the old days that when people died, their souls traveled along the path of the Milky Way back to the south from where they came.

This is a prayer that could be said facing the South:

Great Spirit, You give us life
when we take our food from the Earth, our mother.
We thank you for your gifts.
Keep us from wasting them
and help us remember the needs
of all our relatives,
so that everyone will live healthy lives.

West (Black): This is the direction in which the sun sets and where the day comes to an end. For this reason, it is the direction that stands for the end of life, as Black Elk says: ". . .toward the setting sun of his life." The great Thunderbird lives in the west and it makes thunder and rain come from there. For this reason, the west is the source of water: rain, lakes, streams and rivers. Nothing can live without water, so this direction is very important.

This prayer may be said toward the West:

As the sun sets,
and darkness covers the earth,
we thank you Great Spirit for all your gifts,
especially life-giving water
which keeps us alive.
Cleanse us of all that is evil
and renew us once again.

North (Red): This direction brings the cold, harsh winds of the winter season. These winds are cleansing winds that cause the leaves to fall and the earth to rest under the cover of the snow. If someone has the ability to face these winds like the buffalo with its head into

All mankind is like grass which withers.

I Peter 1:24

the storm, they have learned patience and endurance. Generally, this direction stands for hardships and discomfort to people. Therefore, it stands for trials that people must endure or a cleansing they must undergo.

This prayer is the kind to say while facing the North:

> Great Spirit, we need your strength,
> to help keep us strong,
> in bad times as well as good.
> Help us to be patient
> and wait for your power
> to show us the way to go.
> We rely on your Great Spirit, as we face
> the harsh and purifying winds of life.

When the Lakota pray with the Sacred Pipe, they add two other "directions" to these four: the Sky and the Earth. The Great Spirit, Wakantanka dwells high above like the eagle in the sky and the color of this direction is blue. The Earth is our Mother and Grandmother from whom we receive our nourishment. The color of this direction is green for all growing things.

Depending on the place and the local tradition developed there, the colors attributed to the four directions may vary somewhat. For instance, sometimes red may be assigned to the East.

Sage and Sweet Grass

These growing things are used constantly by the Lakota in their prayers and rituals. By using them, the whole plant world is brought into praying to the Great Spirit as well.

Sweet Grass: This grass is used as incense by burning it in the form of a braid, or on a fire of hot coals. Its smell is pleasant and sweet to

The earth is full of your creatures.

Psalm 104: 24

everyone present, including the Great Spirit who is looking down on everything. Its meaning is to bring down God's blessing on those who are praying and to send upward a visible prayer.

Sage: This herb is used in many ways in the sacred rituals. It is spread around the floor of the sweatlodge, used as a resting place at the center of the clearing during a vision quest, as the resting place for the buffalo skull at times, and when it is burned, it is said to keep evil away. When it is burning, it smells bitter/sweet.

Tobacco: Tobacco is often wrapped in colored cloth and tied to an altar place or other sacred places. The four sacred colors are used for these. This is done as an offering and can stand for a promise or a request of the Great Spirit. Tobacco is also smoked in the Sacred Pipe and its smoke rises up as a visible prayer. It is like "visible breath."

The Eagle

The eagle is a winged symbol for the Lakota people. It is the strongest and bravest of all the birds. For this reason, the eagle and its feathers have been chosen as a symbol of what is highest, bravest, strongest and holiest. Its feathers are given to another to honor them and they are worn with dignity and pride. They are treated with great respect and when one is dropped during a dance, a special ceremony is performed to pick it up again and the owner of it is careful never to drop it again.

It is also used to adorn the sacred pipe because it is a symbol of the Great Spirit who is above all and from whom all strength and power comes.

Eagle feathers or wings are used in special ways. When they are held over someone's head, this means that the person is brave or that he is wished bravery or happiness. To wave it over everyone present is meant that everyone is wished peace, happiness, prosperity and a desire to help them get these things.

Those who trust in God for help,
will find their strength renewed.
They will rise on wings like eagles,
they will run and not grow weary,
they will walk and not grow weak.

Isaiah 40:31

The Buffalo

The buffalo is held in high regard by the Lakota people. It was also respected as a symbol of the divine, because the buffalo was a "banquet" for the people. It gave up its own flesh and life to feed them. It provided for every need of theirs by way of sheltering them with its hide over their tipis, covering their bodies as clothing and their feet as moccasins. It also provided everyday utensils such as needle and thread, and hoes to dig with. In this way, it was a true "relative" for them, making life possible.

For this reason, the symbol of the buffalo and the buffalo skull is present in the sacred rituals of the Lakota. It is there as a reminder of this great animal that gives completely of itself for others. It is a symbol of self-sacrifice. It gives until there is nothing left and it was imitated by the people in their lives. To be generous and give what you have to others in need or to honor them, is one of the most highly respected ways of acting and being.

The Four Values

Generosity (Wacantognaka): Generosity is something that any real Lakota person has. They learn to provide for their family members and relatives, as well as the needy ones in the community. Therefore, a person is looked up to not only for their ability to provide food,

Good will come to him who is generous.   **Psalm 112: 5**

Stand firm and be men of courage.   I Corinthians 16:13

Walk in his ways and reverence Him.   **Deuteronomy 8: 6**

With humility comes wisdom.   Proverbs 11: 2

clothing and shelter, but also for the ability to give generously and not count the cost. It is better to give a lot than to have a lot and keep it for yourself. To be called "stingy" is the worst insult. When an important occasion comes along, people honor one another with a "giveaway" or **otuhan.** During this giveaway, the giver gives much of what he has to other people. Sometimes everything is given away.

Courage (Woohitika): Taking care of others means that a person needs to have bravery or courage. It means having to face hard and difficult things for the sake of others. Therefore, a person is taught by example and stories how to have great courage. They learn to face danger without running away, and how to face even death with dignity. (In the old days, counting coup was a way of proving you had courage.) Today, a person has to have great courage to face bad thoughts and desires inside himself. It takes courage to make changes instead of running away from problems. Any person who does something dangerous to help another is worthy of honor and respect.

Respect (Wowacintanka): In order for people to live together in peace, they have to respect one another. The old are respected for their wisdom and the young because they are the future of the people. This attitude also means a reverence for all other living things in the world. Everything was put on this "island" earth by the Great Spirit. All people and things are relatives. Everything is one, the holy men tell us. This reverence is expressed in daily prayers and by the way we act. The outcome of this respect is peace in families, among tribes and other people. "Although I die, I continue living in everything that is. . .each thing is everything forever," an old Indian once said. We are all one.

Wisdom (Woksape): The knowledge and wisdom of the old people is very important for the well-being of the people. They know how to give "good advice" to others because they have seen many things happen and change. This kind of wisdom helps people get along and understand the world around them. This wisdom helps us see that people are more valuable than things or money. The real way to judge a person is to see inside him. Wisdom is knowing that a person is nothing without the power of God. Being humble, and caring for others is the wisest power of all. Wisdom is like the sun who rises at dawn — we see things the way they are then. This is why traditional people face the dawn each day to pray and ask God to make them wise.

The Circle

The Lakota believe that the circle or hoop is one of the really great symbols, since it can be seen everywhere in the world. The sun is round and the moon is round. It came as no surprise to their ancestors that even the earth was round, like a ball. The seasons come and go, each one following the other like a great circle.

The homes of the traditional people were round like the things in nature. Their tipis were made from a circle of poles, and the whole village was a wider circle made up of these small tipi circles. That is one of the reasons that the life of the people is called the "hoop" or circle of the nation. There is also a deeper reason for that. The life of the people is like a great circle without end. Young ones are born, grow up, become old and then die, and soon more young ones are born to take the place of the old ones. Lame Deer has some words about all this:

> With us the circle stands for the
> togetherness of people who sit with
> one another around a fire,
> relatives and friends united in peace, while
> the pipe passes from hand to hand.
>
> . . .all the families in the village
> were in turn circles within a larger circle,
> part of the larger hoop of the nation.

The Medicine Wheel

The nation was only a part
of the universe, in itself circular. . .
circles within circles within circles,
with no beginning
and no end.

To us this is beautiful and fitting,
symbol and reality at the same time,
expressing the harmony of nature and life.
Our circle is timeless, flowing;
it is new life emerging from death —
life winning out over death.

Medicine Wheel

This belief in the importance of the circle leads naturally to a consideration of the medicine wheel which is a symbol that is very sacred to the Lakota people. It brings together everything they believe about their spiritual life into one symbol. In it you can see the circle which stands for the Great Spirit who has no beginning and no end, the entire life of the people and creation, and the four directions which are represented by the cross. Very often an eagle feather is attached to this sacred wheel making the strength and beauty of the Great Spirit an even closer part of this symbol.

One is reminded of the passage in scripture which speaks of the circular aspect of life:

A generation goes, a generation comes.
The sun rises, the sun sets.
Southward goes the wind, then turns to the north,
it turns and turns again
back to its circling goes the wind.

Ecclesiastes 1: 4-7

The Family Circle

The symbol of the circle also introduces us to the concept of family. This may seem odd at first, but it becomes clearer to us if we use the familiar term of **family circle.** The traditional Lakota family circle is called the **tiyospaye** and can be translated as extended family. It is a concept that includes aunts and uncles, grandmothers and grandfathers, as well as cousins and those who have been incorporated into the family through marriage. As Christians, we may recall the passage from the Gospels in which Jesus cannot be found after the family's visit to the temple in Jerusalem. His parents' immediate response is to search for him among the other relatives — the extended family. Jesus was brought up within a wide circle of relatives. For the biblical world and the Lakota world life is a matter of circles within circles. One is a member of an immediate family, then a wider circle of relatives, and finally the entire nation. Beyond that group of familiars there exists the world of animals and spirits, plants and rocks which are also considered to be relatives. One addresses each of these in its own proper way, while Wakantanka is worthy of the greatest respect. Thus the concept is one of a cohesive, harmonious organism: Life. "All my relatives" becomes the great prayer which expresses this reality of interrelated beings. It is an apparently simple expression, but very profound to those who understand.

The Morning Star

There is a star that stands alone in the sky and shines very brightly in the east just before the sun comes up. This star is called the "Morning Star" by the Lakota. It is the star that announces the coming of the sun and its light on the earth. For this reason, it is very important to the people and is used often in their designs and decorations.

Black Elk talks about this star as a bringer of wisdom to men

Send out your light and your truth.

Psalm 43

because it announces the bright daylight of knowledge which enables the world to see its way more clearly. That is why this star is regarded as sacred, because of the function it has been given by the Creator as a herald.

The Sun

The sun is the greatest symbol of the Great Spirit, Wakantanka. This is so because it is the light which brightens the whole world and which causes things to live and to grow. Along with the sacred tree, it is one of the main symbols of the sundance ceremony. Throughout this ceremony which is held during the summer, when the sun is its hottest, the dancers regard its path in the sky, honoring it as it goes from East to West. Its shape is round like the circle which has no beginning or end. It rises and sets day after day, always repeating the same cycle. It is the source of life, drawing the growing things up from the soil of the earth by its warm rays and is one of the greatest creative forces in the universe. It shares powerfully in God's ongoing creation of the world and therefore has first place among the symbols.

This is a prayer to the Great Spirit of the Sun:

Father, Great Spirit,
You are the center of our lives,
and we look to you for all that
we need to stay alive.
If you shine on us
and bless us, we are happy.
If you hide your face,
we are helpless without you,
and we perish from the face of the earth.
Bless and keep us
and all people who honor you.

Mother Earth

The Lakota have unique concepts of the earth — Mother Earth — and the spirituality surrounding rocks and stones — Inyan. The earth is sacred to the Lakota because it is the mother of all living things. It provides food for all living creatures, nurturing them constantly. From the earth, the altars at the various ceremonies are made by scraping a clearing or scooping the dirt into a small mound. It is customary to sit on the ground in closeness to this Mother, and it is one of the six directions toward which the Sacred Pipe is pointed in prayer.

For the Lakota people, the Black Hills or He Sapa as they have called them for generations, hold a special place on this earth and in their spirituality. They are also referred to as the "center of everything that is" and have been a place of prayer and spiritual renewal for hundreds, perhaps thousands of years. Its high peaks have been the site of many a vision quest and fast, and its earth contains the dust of their ancestors who have been buried there. It is understandable that these sacred hills have a meaning for them which is difficult for others to understand. In the old days, they were regarded with such great awe and respect that the people never lived in them, but only visited them to pray, cut tipi poles and bury their dead.

The Rock

The Rock — Inyan — is the oldest thing that can be found on the earth. It also has a sacredness which belongs to it in the Lakota spirituality and it is the stones and rocks which figure prominently in the sweatlodge. When the water is poured over the heated rocks, they give off the steam which is so beneficial to body and spirit. It is the red stone which is dug up from the earth that is made into the bowl of the sacred pipe and is therefore an essential element in Lakota spirituality. Stones also communicate to mankind with a

I will lift up my eyes to the hills.   **Psalm 121**

message which is completely their own. Their message and meaning are for those who know how to be open and listen.

It was said about the old people of the Lakota that they "worshipped rocks." It is true that they had special large rocks which they used to go to and pray. But these stones were regarded as a way of getting in touch with the spirit: God. The Lakota people could think of nothing more ancient than the rocks. They were here before anything or anyone else. No one could remember time or history before the rocks. Therefore, the stones and rocks at which they prayed reminded them of "Tunkashila" — Grandfather. They called God their Grandfather because, like the rocks, he always existed before them.

Spiritual Messengers

The **spirits** which are helpers on behalf of the Lakota people are a very important aspect of Lakota spirituality. They come and go between invisible and visible worlds bringing messages of guidance and wisdom to those who are seeking these with humility. They sometimes manifest themselves during a ceremony such as the sweatlodge. Often they come as a helper to the person who is fasting and praying alone on a hill-top.

This topic of "spirits" is a very delicate one, however, since there are many Lakota Christians who feel rather uncomfortable when talking about it. They often feel these things are not to be spoken about too much since dealing with the spirits is a mysterious and sometimes dangerous matter. Ultimately, it is something that the Lakota need to work out for themselves since few outside the Lakota experience are able to understand it as well as they or decide for them how they are to interpret the meaning and phenomena of the spirits.

The souls of the good are in the hand of God. To the foolish they seem to be dead, but they are in peace. **Wisdom 3:1-3**

Death

In the Lakota tradition, which is part of nature and closely observes the signs and seasons in nature, life and death are one never-ending circle. The sun "dies" each day to be born again in the morning. Plants wither in the cold of winter only to rise up from the earth in the spring. So it is with people — the spirits of those who die travel the path to where all the loved ones have gone before them. Those who seem dead are really alive and have gone to another place.

In the old days, Lakota did not bury their dead under the ground. They put them on a scaffold or in a tree so that they could return easily to the wind and sky, as well as the earth. They were laid to rest with some of their favorite things: shields, drums, moccasins, medicine bundles or even their favorite horse. Sometimes all their possessions were given away, or the family members, in grief, gave away all that they owned to others, stripping themselves of everything. After one year, on the anniversary of their death, a memorial meal was held and there was a giveaway in honor of the dead person. Some traditional Lakota also put aside a little piece of food in honor of the dead at meals since love and communication can go beyond death. Tattooing a little design on their own hand or wrist was done to serve as a mark of admission into the spirit world when it came their turn to die, and pass over the bridge to the next life.

Black Elk spoke about facing death with courage, yet seeing it as a normal part of life.

He said that it is good to have a reminder of death before us, for it helps us understand that life on this earth will not last forever, and this may help us to prepare for our own death.

Ask the animals and they will teach you.   Job 12: 7

Animals

"The animals speak to us," the Lakota say. Sometimes if a person is willing to listen and look quietly, animals will come around and bring a message. It might be a little bird in the top of a tree, a rabbit hopping by, or even an ant. Even a prairie dog who pops his head out of his hole may have something to tell us. If these animals are not respected, like the buffalo, they may disappear from the earth. Then the Lakota and all people will be without their message forever.

Animals were created by the Great Spirit first, before people were put on the earth. In this way, they are closer to God, helping to get the earth ready for people to live in. They were told to sacrifice themselves for others that people might have something to eat. The Lakota always offer an apology for killing their relatives, the animals, and pray in thanksgiving for the food they give.

Animals are also very simple and pure. They always do whatever God has made them to do. They are not going around doing bad things to their own kind. They have their own code put in them by the Great Spirit, and they always live according to that code. In the fall, the geese know it is time to come together and fly south. Animals are kind to their little ones and protect them by putting themselves in danger. They only take and use what they need to survive.

Animals are relatives of the human beings and as such, are part of the great web of life where each thing is dependent on the other. As relatives, they are worthy of respect.

The Lakota Code

Love one another.

Pity orphan children. Be kind to them because they are poor, feed them and clothe them.

Do not kill one another.

Do not steal anything from anyone, especially from your own people.

Do not tell lies to anyone, or lie about anyone.

Respect your brothers and sisters. Do not marry in your own family.

The ability to make good speech is a great gift from their maker, owner of all things, to the people. This is why you should not talk badly about anyone. Bad talk can hurt one's family or everyday life.

Never quarrel among one another. Be good to others and always be friendly to whomever you meet, wherever you meet them.

Do not brag about yourself, or try to hurt another's feelings. The generous person is the one who is respected.

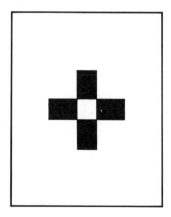

Chapter 3

Vatican II

Once the liturgy of the Catholic Church had been revised by the Second Vatican Council, there were some people who felt that it should no longer be tampered with. There are still some people who feel that we now have a "catholic" or universal liturgy and that it should remain as it is. These same people want to give the impression that the Roman Rite is the universal rite, fulfilling the needs of all people in all places.

In fact, the Roman Rite is intentionally an example of brevity and simplicity. These very qualities make adaptation to the cultural needs of local churches possible. This is exactly what the council fathers had in mind when they revised it. Rigid uniformity was never their intention.

In the **Constitution on the Liturgy,** they set guidelines and conditions for the admission of elements from other cultures and traditions into the worship of the local churches. Those elements of the liturgy that are divinely instituted may not be changed, for they have been established by Jesus himself. Other elements, however, are subjects for change since they are added by men (SC 21). Therefore, the use of water and the invocation of the Trinity during Baptism are immutable, whereas elements such as candles and white garments are changeable. In the Eucharist, the words of consecration are immutable, while vestments, music and language are changeable. Sections 37-40 of the Constitution guide those attempting this process of adapting liturgy to a particular culture. What elements may be used? The document states:

> Anything in these peoples' way of life that is not indissolubly bound up with superstition and error, she studies

and if possible preserves intact. She sometimes even admits such things into the liturgy itself, as long as they harmonize with its true and authentic spirit (SC 37).

This guideline is applicable to a broad range of material such as sacramentals, processions, language, music and art. In answer to the question: who has the task of deciding how and what elements are to be admitted? SC 40 states clearly that it is the bishop of the area who determines:

> . . .which elements from the traditions and genius of indivu-al peoples might appropriately be admitted into divine wor-ship.

One begins to understand with the aid of these guidelines how vastly different the liturgy might appear when it is thoroughly adapted to a particular culture, using the music, art, language, dance and sacramentals of that culture. Perhaps Native American liturgy would employ drummers and singers doing their traditional songs and right-ly so.

> There are people who have their own musical tradition, and this plays a great part in their religious and social life. For this reason, their music should be held in proper esteem and a suitable place be given to it, not only in forming their religious sense but also in adapting worship to their native genius (SC 119).

A Native American liturgy might also have a "grand entry" with the participants dressed in bells, feathers and beadwork. Sweet grass and cedar might be burned as incense, with eagle feathers held aloft over the people as a blessing. Prayers might be offered to God as the

Great Spirit and a recognition of the Four Spirits who dwell in the Four Directions of the universe.

The Church is universal and welcomes the cultural expression of all nations in praise of God the creator of all.

> The Church has not adopted any particular style of art as her own; art from every race and region shall also be given free scope provided that it adorns the sacred buildings and holy rites with due reverence and honor (SC 123).

The key to successfully introducing culture into the life of the church is **instruction** of the people and **reflection** with them. Adaptation and reflection go hand in hand. In this way, there is no confusion in the minds of the people in the community and the Christian meaning is made clear to them. Nothing should be introduced unless it has been re-oriented to Christ and explained theologically to the people.

It must involve **authentic** culture — it must express what the people experience in reality. This is another way of saying that there should not be any split between the life of the people and their deepest values on one hand, and their manner of worship on the other. They ought to worship God as only they know how, as people uniquely fashioned by their Creator. It would be a disservice to themselves and an affront to their Creator to borrow a way of worshipping from another culture and to disown their own ways. God had desired **this** people to glorify Him with their own music, song, dance, symbols and language.

Also, it is important to remember that "the people" have a great deal to say about what goes into the making of a Lakota Mass or liturgy if it is to be local worship. If they are not comfortable with the introduction of a particular item or objects, or if they do not feel that an action, a gesture or a song is appropriate, then attention must be given to this opinion. Ultimately, the entire community — and the people as an integral part of it — are the test whether or not something is working.

Another point to remember in dealing with the religious heritage of the Lakota, is really a word of caution. Many Lakota seem uncomfortable with incorporating what is part of a sacred rite from their heritage into the liturgy or sacraments. For instance, some feel it would not be appropriate to "mix" religions in a way that would combine the rituals of baptism and inipi (sweatlodge) even though there may be many common elements in both, such as the use of water as cleansing.

Many Christian Lakota would prefer that if there is to be a pipe ceremony that it take place either before or after a ritual such as the liturgy, rather than during it. It is not that one militates against the other, it's just that they regard each ritual as having its proper place. They are different and ought to remain different, not blended, they say. Perhaps too much mixing would water down the effect of each, for power resides in both the Lakota and the Christian rituals, but each in their own way.

Besides the Decree on the Liturgy, Vatican Council II also produced a document concerning the relationship that properly ought to exist between the church and the religions which are not Christian. In English, it has the long title of **"The Relations of the Church to Non-Christian Religions."** The Lakota spirituality or "Indian religion" as it is sometimes called, can be approached by church members with the help of these guidelines. They are general but can and ought to have very specific and local influence. Christians are encouraged to examine the Lakota spirituality and whatever they find to be true and holy in it, they are asked to respect.

The Catholic Church rejects nothing of what is true and holy in these religions. (#2)

A sun and a shield is the Lord God.   **Psalm 84: 12**

Christians — both Lakota and non-Lakota who are working among the Lakota — are urged to not only **tolerate,** but even **promote** the good they discover existing within the Lakota religious heritage.

> Let Christians acknowledge, preserve and encourage the spiritual and moral truths found among non-Christians, also their social life and culture. (#2)

These are positive, non-destructive goals for the clergy and laity both on and off the reservation, who are involved in working with the Lakota. These words are also an encouragement for those Lakota who continue to struggle with their traditional identity as people of the "good red road" while trying to follow the way of Christ as believers in his Gospel.

Vatican II also gave its attention to the efforts of those members of the church who are called missionaries. We no longer tend to regard the Lakota country as "mission country" because much of it has been Christian for over a century now. The vast majority of Lakota have membership in one of the Christian denominations, be it Roman Catholic or Episcopal. The document **On Missionary Activity** (Ad Gentes), however, does lend some further insight into the importance of local culture in the process of preaching the Gospel. Once again, native culture is to be respected, not destroyed. It is taken for granted that the Gospel is not necessarily bound to western European culture but is able to be adapted to any culture in the world.

The (new) Christian community

> . . .must be deeply rooted in the people (who) live for God and Christ according to the honorable usages of their race. (#5)

The Lakota Christian community — we may say Lakota church — is asked to:

. . .borrow from the customs, traditions, wisdom, teaching
and arts of their people, everything which could be used
to praise the glory of the Creator. (#22)

This is not an easy task, but must be understood as involving a
great deal of prayer and thought on the part of all members of this
native church. It means that a thorough examination of the culture
and the influence of the Gospel needs to occur:

. . .theological investigation should be encouraged and the
facts and words revealed by God, contained in scripture and
explained by the Church, submitted to a new examination in
the light of the tradition of the universal Church. (#22)

All of this ought to take place so that the message of the Gospel can
be announced and explained in terms which the Lakota people can
appreciate and feel "at home."

Thus a way will be opened for a more profound adaptation (and) the Christian life will be adapted to the mentality
and character of each culture. (#22)

This document provides further for a sound and thorough preparation for those who intend to work amidst a culture other than their
own. The message is very important for those non-Lakota persons
who want to enter the Lakota milieu. They may have all the goodwill
and sincerity in the world but lack cultural sensitivity. As the saying
goes: "deliver us from sincere people." This means that zealous persons may do more harm than good if they are not intelligent about
their efforts. They may even equip themselves with a little knowledge
about Lakota ways and culture, and then become dangerous to the
spiritual well-being of the local community of believers. To inflict
these Lakota believers with a sense of cultural inferiority would be

I want to gather you under my wings. **Luke 13:34**

harmful and a denial of the positive affirmation which they ought to receive in the Gospel message, that they are valuable in the eyes of God. According to the document:

> Whoever is to go among another people must hold their inheritance, language and way of life in great esteem. (#26)

The priest, deacon, sister or catechist ought to study carefully the ways of the people God has called them to serve. They should regard their ways with respect, doing this realistically, not romantically. They are the ways of a real people with real needs. They should apply themselves to this study for a reasonable length of time:

> . . .that they might understand more fully the history, social structures and customs of the people, that they might have an insight into their moral outlook, their religious precepts and the intimate ideas which they form of God, the world and men according to their own sacred traditions. (#26)

The minister of the Gospel who states that he or she doesn't need to know about culture but "only Christ" is in danger of jeopardizing the very Gospel they have set out to preach, for without realizing it, they may be introducing their own values and western culture which have nothing to do with the essential message of the Gospel. A story is to be told of an early missionary among the Lakota who set up a chapel in their midst and began holding services. The people who came to witness these services entered the chapel and sat around the altar in a circle as was their custom at any gathering. Whenever they heard something that touched them or met with their agreement or admiration, they uttered "Han!" Later on, after this initial encounter, the priest informed them that their behavior was not "proper" for worship in church. Thereafter, they attended church quietly, facing the altar in rows. The Gospel has nothing to do with lining up in rows, yet unwittingly the priest confused his own values with the message of Christ, thereby stifling the spirit.

Unfortunately, perhaps, the Lakota learned their lessons too well, so that to this day, worshipping in a circle during the liturgy is an uncomfortable, "unchurchy" experience. Many of them would much rather stand in rows facing the altar. Perhaps in another one hundred years they will once more be gathered around the meal of Christ in the restored, sacred circle.

Paul and the Jesuits

The history of evangelization in the Church affords us many examples or models of how the Gospel was or was not adapted to a particular cultural setting. Two examples of how the Gospel was adapted are offered for our consideration here: the Pauline model in the early Church and the Jesuit model which is closer to our time in the 17th century. Both were precursors of the Second Vatican Council.

The Pauline Model. One of the great debates which concerned the early Church was the one between Gentile and Jewish believers in Christ. Many of the Jewish believers saw their acceptance of Jesus as an extension of their Jewish faith and tradition, and wanted to continue worshipping in Jewish ways as well as circumcizing and obeying the Torah. They felt that they were still Jews just as Jesus had been a Jew and had announced the Gospel to them first. In **Acts** 15, we read about the confrontation which took place between those who insisted that the Jewish elements must be continued and those who felt that belief in the Gospel had nothing to do with the Jewish traditions anymore. Paul often addressed this issue in his letters, especially **Romans, Galatians** and **Colossians,** and he even boasted about his Jewish roots: "Are they Israelites? So am I!" In **Romans** 11, he reminds his readers that it is not possible that God has rejected his chosen people, because He never goes back on his word. He calls the new Gentile Christians "grafted branches":

> . . .like shoots of wild olive, you have been grafted among the rest to share with the rich sap provided by the olive tree itself. **Romans 11: 17-18**

Some of Paul's remarks about Gentiles not needing to practice the Jewish traditions may sound like an argument against our contention that Lakota customs and spirituality are not to be rejected. His solution to the problem is actually one that is applicable to the Lakota situation, however. He offers every respect to their tradition as he leads the new Jewish converts to Christ's message of forgiveness, but he also makes it clear that this Jewish tradition is not for everyone. For the Jewish Christians, it is important that they remember that their roots are deep in Judaism and the Torah. For the Gentile Christians, it is equally important for them to remember the great debt owed to the Jewish traditions of Abraham, Moses and the Torah, but they are not bound by the forms of worship, rituals and customs of this tradition. In other words, Paul's solution is one of "live and let live." In the end, it is the forgiveness of God in Christ which saves them both: Gentile and Jew.

Paul encountered many other problems and situations in his newly founded Christian communities such as Corinth. His letters to that Christian community provide us with an example of how he admitted elements into Christian worship that were "pre-Christian." One such element was the phenomenon of "glossalaly" or **tongues,** as it is called. Apparently the Corinthians who were recent converts from various cults and mystery religions were experiencing ecstatic utterances during their prayer services. Christians who were not accustomed to this style of praying and the excitement it engendered were concerned about it and appealed to Paul for advice. Paul recognized that these new Christians were using a prayer form that arose from their pre-Christian background and was able to accept this religious expression into the native church at Corinth.

Praying in "tongues" or "glossalaly" was a phenomenon which had a parallel in the non-Christian religious milieu of Corinth. Worshippers were seized with emotion and fervor, and under the influence of the divine encounter, began making utterances which were unintelligible to the others present, as if it were another language. It is from this phenomenon that our word "enthusiasm" is derived, since the Greek "en theos" means "in god." Paul then, recognized it as a valid way of praying, grounded it in a Christian meaning, and specified certain regulations concerning it. It was to be allowed only when there was someone present who could act as an interpreter, and reverence and good order were to be maintained at all times. Thus, Paul accepted it and called it a spiritual gift for the service of the local church.

The Jesuit Model

When the Jesuit missionaries began preaching the Gospel among the Native Americans in the northeast area of the United States and Canada in the early 1600's, they used a method that had been tried by other Jesuit missionaries in South American areas, China and elsewhere. It entailed bringing the Gospel to indigenous people without imposing inflexible modes of worship and codes of conduct. Rather than condemn the culture which they encountered as pre-Christian, they examined it carefully, learning the language and customs while living among the people as one of them. They attempted to find the common ground and build on that, and as they moved among the people, they tried not to damage their economic structures, social structures and spiritual values. They wanted the Native American identity to remain intact as new Christians, and, the converts' culture profoundly affected the lives of the missionaries themselves, both inwardly and outwardly. The Jesuits, like Jean de Brebeuf, revised the Gospel message to fit the Huron culture and their ability to understand it. They went to great efforts to maintain the local customs — some of them religious — which were not regarded as contrary to the message of Christ. The great Feast of the Dead which was so important to the Hurons in order to maintain kinship with family members both living and dead, was attended and even encouraged by the Jesuits. Later on, this love for the deceased and the desire to join them one day, was incorporated into their preaching so that those who lived good lives were encouraged by the prospect of joining their family members after death. The sweatlodge was not only tolerated but allowed and encouraged as another way to pray to the Creator.

They made every effort to train native catechists and preachers so that the Gospel could be heard in the native tongue and in the idiom and turn of phrase which was so familiar to the listeners. These native preachers drew on a solid oratorical tradition which was put to skillful service on behalf of the message of Christ. Many other customs were heartily encouraged such as dancing to celebrate feast days such as Easter which was understood as the "victory dance" of Christ over evil. Gift-giving was a natural partner of the "sharing of all things in common" that was the custom during the early days of the Christian community.

The Jesuits wanted to see to it that the new Christians were able to live a thoroughly Christian life without suffering any cultural disintegration. In fact, they sometimes went to great lengths to remove any European influence which more often than not had a negative influence on the people. This was the process of "assimilation" in the other direction, meaning that the Gospel was assimilated into the Indian culture. Their goal was not the Europeanization of the Native American people and they sought to distinguish between what was essential in the Gospel and what was only culturally and historically European and therefore, non-essential. The very death of

The sacrifice acceptable to God is a humble spirit.   **Psalm 51**

a man like Jean de Brebeuf was an example of cultural adaptation since he determined to die in the courageous manner of a warrior, neither crying out during his torture nor pleading for mercy as the most unspeakable things were done to his body. His captors did not miss the point since the account of his martyrdom comes from Native American eye-witnesses.

Keeping in mind the guidelines of the Second Vatican Council and surveying the history of how the Gospel has been preached at various times and finally the example of Jesus Himself, it becomes clear that adapting the liturgy and Gospel message to the Lakota culture is not an **option.** In fact, heeding the words of Jesus to his contemporaries, we too ought to discern the "signs of the times." It is apparent for those who "have eyes to see and ears to hear" that the Lakota people are struggling to maintain their identity and culture in the midst of all sorts of difficulties and pressures, both from without their communities and from within. They seem to be doing this with ever increasing strength, however, as the traditional ways regain vitality at a time when others have assumed they have lost their power. Non-Indian influences have attempted to suppress this culture and spirituality over many years and have been unsuccessful in bringing about the assimilation of native peoples into the mainstream of American values. Traditional ceremonies, values and customs have re-surfaced again over the last few years.

It is now apparent that these traditional ways and values as interpreted through religious acts were never totally eradicated by either the government or the churches which were at various times hostile powers arrayed against them. This trend or revival of Lakota spirituality and religious expression seems to be growing and unless the people who are spreading the Gospel in native localities are willing to have an open mind and are willing to change with the times, they will lose out in the end — or rather the Gospel of Jesus is in danger of losing. It is vitally important for the Church to adapt, or young people and others who are reviving their heritage will not find a home within the Church. The Church needs to discern in which direction the wind of the Spirit is blowing and begin moving in that direction.

Furthermore, adaptation is not something novel and untried, for it was the method of the Lord himself when he joined our human race as a member of the Jewish community and family. Jesus took to himself, as the Son of God, a particular culture. His was a body with Jewish blood flowing through his veins, Jewish language flowing from his lips. He had family ties and customs among a specific people. The Jewish spiritual tradition of Abraham, Moses and the covenant was his source of inspiration, for the Torah was his to study as a young man and to quote as a rabbi during his public life. His love for the Temple was unquestionable, surpassing the attitude of his contemporaries who stood back as he cleared it of animals and money in order to restore it as a place of prayer.

It was the will of God that the Gospel first appear among humanity through the mediation of one particular man as a member of one particular culture. The lesson of this incarnation ought not to be lost for us. It is a lesson in **cultural acceptance.** We who are the faithful followers of the Lord ought to be open to every culture in which we are trying to live the Gospel. Jesus' method ought to be our method, and our love for Him ought to fill us with a zeal to celebrate his message in a similar manner in the Lakota way.

"In the days to come I will pour out my spirit on all mankind." **Joel 3: 1-5**

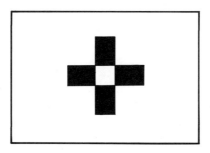

Chapter 4

Culture and the Gospel

Since culture is a term with which we are concerned throughout this book, we might well ask, what exactly is culture? We will use the following definition:

> Culture is the entirety of a people's expression of life according to their art, music, language, rituals and beliefs, oral and written traditions, especially their values.

The culture of any given group of people is an expression of what they value — what they hold to be precious and ideal. Culture as such, does not mean the failures of individual people to uphold these values and ideals. This is especially important to remember when encountering the aspects of a people's day-to-day life that show the deterioration of values or the failure of culture caused by outside pressures. Alcoholism and the disruption of family life may be prevalent in a society or location but this is not a result of their culture. This is evidence of the stress that the people are experiencing as they encounter challenges to their cultural identity from without.

We have the example of Jesus himself with regard to using the local cultures, in both Baptism and the Eucharist. Jesus participated in these two ancient — pre-Christian, if you will — rituals and deepened their meaning for those of us who were to follow after Him. It was Jesus' command to go forth and baptize "in the name of the Father, Son and Holy Spirit" that transformed the ritual of Baptism. The origin of the Eucharist is found in the Jewish **seder** and **berakah.** It was during the Passover meal on the night before He died that Jesus took the bread and wine and drew out from these the meaning of his sacrificial death. His sacrifice continues to sustain us in this memorial meal we call our Eucharist.

The anointing of the sick and the imposition of hands are also signs and customs in which the members of the early Church participated according to the example of Jesus himself. The entire Old Testament is a body of pre-Christian literature and was accepted as having a deeper meaning and therefore re-oriented to Christ by the early church members. Prime examples of this process of understanding are the Psalms in which the meaning of "Lord" is often given over to Christ. Besides the Passover, another Jewish festival that was profoundly influential with Christian theology was Yom Kippur or Day of Atonement. The atonement theology has perdured for centuries in the church's thinking concerning the explanation of Christ's redemptive suffering on behalf of "the many." It was his blood which was understood then as covering the sins of humanity and which won the mercy of God. The Letter to the Hebrews is a marvelous example of inculturation at work, as it uses the concepts of temple, holy of holies, priesthood, offerings and covenant in a new and transformed manner. Everything in the former temple and its services is now related to Christ and his accomplishment of redemption.

If there is respect for and accommodation of the local culture, a fruitful exchange develops whereby the tradition of the culture is enhanced by the spirit of Christ, and the Gospel message and the church are enriched in turn. In this marvelous exchange, Christ receives the glory of native followers worshipping Him in their unique ways. The liturgy of the Easter vigil sings about the "wondrous exchange" that takes place between God and humanity!

A wonderful exchange is evident between Christ and the Lakota culture in the following brief outline of symbols and figures.

Christian	Lakota
1. Praying with the mystical body and all creation, as in Francis of Assisi's "Canticle of the Sun." All angels and saints join in praising God.	Praying in the presence of all creation: "All my relatives" as well as all good spirits who serve the Great Spirit, Wakantanka.
2. The Mass as a memorial meal of the Last Supper and Jesus' death.	The memorial meal on the anniversary of the death of a loved one.
3. The courage of the martyrs and saints, reverence for life, the Gospel message of "give and you shall receive," the wisdom of God's ways.	The values of courage, respect, generosity and wisdom.
4. The 10 Commandments.	The Lakota code.
5. Cleansing ourselves in Baptism as we seek a new life in God. Renewing ourselves in the Rite of Reconciliation.	Purifying the mind and body in the sweatlodge to perform God's will better.
6. The example and words of Christ: "Deny yourself, take up your cross and follow me."	Sundance as an act of self-sacrifice on behalf of the people, "that they might live."

7. Symbols of the Divine: Circle Sun Eagle Burning Bush Holy Spirit	Symbols of the Divine: Circle Sun Eagle Signs in Nature Great Spirit
8. Morning Star Facing the East (our churches).	Morning Star Facing the East to pray.
9. A woman brings the Prince of Peace: Jesus.	A woman brings the message of Peace: the Pipe.
10. The soul lives on after the body dies.	The soul lives on after the body dies.
11. Incense as a symbol of prayer.	Sweet grass, tobacco as visible prayer.
12. Prayer of individual as sinful before God's holiness, the need for mercy: Lord have mercy!	Prayer of the person alone before the Great Spirit: Have pity on me! Without you I am nothing!

Re-orientation

It is apparent then, that one of the principles involved with expressing the Gospel in a culture such as the Lakota culture is the process of **re-orientation.** In order for cultural elements to be maintained for Christian use, they must undergo a certain process whereby the Christian comes to a deeper understanding of them. Another way of saying this is that they need to be understood in the light of Christ and

He was in the world, and through Him the world was made.
John 1:10

receive further meaning from Him. Perhaps in some cases, it is simply a matter of evaluating the thing in question and coming to the realization that it is not hostile to the Gospel message, but actually supports it and complements it.

In the historical account of Chief Gall's conversion to Christianity by Ella Deloria in **Speaking of Indians,** we find this process of re-orientation taking place as Gall struggles to understand the meaning of Wakantanka, the Great Spirit, as the Father of Jesus. Gall spent many Sunday services sitting in the humblest place by the door of the mission church on his reservation. There he listened to the preaching of the missionary, scrutinizing every word that he spoke as he explained the meaning of the Gospel to the congregation. Finally, Gall called the missionary to his home and gave a banquet in his honor, during which he explained his conclusions about the Gospel of Jesus:

> What you tell us this man Jesus says, we must do unto others, I already know. Be kind to your neighbor, feed him, be better to him than to yourself, he says. Of course! Aren't we all Dakotas? Members one of another, he says. My younger brother, do you know of any group of Dakota people who are not linked together in kinship? If anyone wants you to escort him part way, take him to his very tipi door. If he asks for your shirt, by all means give him your blanket also, he says. Well, all that I have always done and I know it is good. But now he says, love your enemies, for they are your brothers. And he says, if someone strikes one cheek, let him strike the other, too. That I have never done. That I have to learn, hard as it sounds.
>
> What is entirely new to me is that the Wakan is actually the Father of all men and so he loves even me and wants me to be safe. This man you talk about has made Wakan-tanka very plain to me, whom I only groped for once — in fear. Whereas I once looked about me on a mere level with

my eyes and saw only my fellow man to do him good, now I know how to look up and see God, my Father, too. It is wašte (good).   **(Deloria p. 65-66)**

Gall's concept of Wakantanka has been transformed and made "very plain," so that the foreshadowing now blossomed into the fullness of understanding. It should be noted that belief in Wakantanka has not been destroyed by Christian revelation, but has found its fulfillment in Christianity, according to the promise of Jesus.

The belief in Wakantanka among the Lakota had been a somewhat open-ended one, clouded in mystery as it were. This mysterious concept could be fulfilled in the Christian revelation as it was in the case of Chief Gall, so that the Great Mystery became clearer for the Lakota Christian.

Now God could be understood in a new way and according to custom among the Lakota, when a new stage in life has come, a new name is called for — Ateunyapi (Father).

A good example in Lakota spirituality of how a person can remain fully Lakota and Christian is found in the ritual of the sweatlodge. The sweatlodge is a ritual which emphasizes water in the form of steam as cleansing, and light piercing the darkness just as wisdom enters the lives of humanity to guide them. In this ceremony, the participants purify their bodies as an outward sign of the inward cleansing of their spirits.

A brief review of the elements of the sweatlodge ritual may prove helpful at this point. The sweatlodge itself is made of poles that are covered with hides or blankets, and in the center of the floor a pit contains hot rocks. When the participants have gathered around the interior of the sweatlodge, the flap is closed and water is poured over the rocks, creating a bath of steam. Prayers are offered for cleansing and the well-being of all present as well as any others the participants wish to pray for. After a while, the flap is opened and light streams in. Water is passed around for all to drink, then the flap is closed again and the process begins over again. It happens in this way until the leader has prayed to all Four Directions of the universe. Each of the directions has its special symbolism: WEST — This is where thunder and rainstorms come from and all creatures owe their lives to this water. NORTH — This is where the powerful winds come from that cleanse us and make us pure as snow. EAST — This is where the morning star is seen and where the sun comes up. In the light we see things wisely. SOUTH — This is where the sun is warmest and from whence life originates. When people die, it is said their souls return in this direction.

When prayers have been said in the last direction, the leader speaks to the participants about opening the flap for the last time, and he tells them that the light which will enter their darkness is like the light of Wakantanka which shines in their minds and hearts.

If we understand the Sweatlodge correctly, we can see that it enables the devout participants to achieve valuable spiritual goals. They cleanse themselves and cleanse their spirits by the water and steam, as well as concentration on the Great Spirit who will help them in their pitiful condition. They pray not only for themselves but for all the people. There is some common ground (commonality) between this rite and the rite of Baptism with the use of water and its cleansing symbolism. The repetition of this rite at certain times during life is more similar perhaps, to the Rite of Reconciliation which is likewise repeated at various times for the sake of cleansing and re-orientation of the spirit to God. The symbolism of light piercing the darkness is also similar to Baptism in which we understand that the Light of Christ comes into our lives. We hold our candles in our hands during this ceremony, which have been lit by the Easter candle, a symbol of Christ. We are given a white garment to symbolize our cleansing from sin. Although our sins were like scarlet, now they are white as snow. We are reminded of the symbolism of the prayer to the North in the sweatlodge. It is the North wind that cleanses and brings the purity of the snows. When the final flap is opened and light enters the sweatlodge, one is reminded of: "The people who were sitting in darkness have seen a great light." **(Luke 1:79)** The rite of **Inipi** or Sweatlodge can also be compared to the opening rite of purification in the Liturgy where themes of water and cleansing are interwoven in the ceremony of the Asperges. (An example of culturally adapting this ceremony is given later in the chapter on liturgy.)

As for the Lakota Christians who participate in the Sweatlodge, the outward expressions of this ritual may not change at all, but by reason of their own faith, the ritual has taken on a deeper meaning — a transformation because of their relationship with Christ. They are able to reflect on the spirituality in the symbols and actions and join with the words of James in their spirits, while their bodies are cleansed:

> Give in to God then,
> resist the evil spirit,
> and he will run away from you.
> The nearer you go to God,
> the nearer He will come to you.
> Wash yourselves and clear your minds.
> Look at your pitiful condition and
> weep for it in misery.
> Humble yourselves before the Lord
> and He will lift you up.

> **James 4: 7-11**

Mitakuye Oyasin (All My Relatives) is a saying that enriches the church as a gift from the spiritual insight and tradition of the Lakota people. It is a marvelously brief but deep expression of what life is. In a few short words, it includes everything spiritual and material, everything seen and unseen, everything that is real. It includes God who is the Great Spirit above all and in all. It includes all his spiritual messengers that move between God and humanity. It includes all the

He lives above the circle of the earth, stretching the sky like a tent for men to live in. **Isaiah 40: 22**

"ancient ones" — those who have died to us but who are now alive to Him and gathered around Him in joy and peace. It includes all men and women, all children who are now living on the face of the earth. It includes all creatures that fly in the air, walk or crawl on the earth or within the earth, and that swim in the waters. It includes the very earth itself and the air that surrounds it like a beautiful blanket.

"All My Relatives" is a saying that recognizes all creation and the Creator as one great family. It extends **kinship** to everything "that lives and moves and has its being." Nothing can happen therefore, to one part of this creation that does not in some small way happen to the rest of creation and its Creator. We are FAMILY whether we realize it or not at times, but the earth always realizes it, and the animals always realize it, and God the Spirit never forgets it. To all of them, our kinsfolk, our family members we owe our very lives, for they support us and keep us in existence. Everything forms a great web of interdependence giving daily, even second by second, what is needed to keep everything alive. The spider-web can serve as a parable for our minds to dwell on, as to what this family can be likened. Everything is interwoven and interdependent. If one part is unraveling, then it begins to weaken the rest of the web. Conversely, if every part is strong and knows its place and what it is to do, then the entire web is strong and healthy. All creation is one, is harmonious and holy. Like the garment of Jesus, it is a continuous weave and must not be torn apart. Every part needs to be reverenced as holy and worthy of respect so that it can have the freedom to carry out its duties and functions. The earth must not be poisoned and scraped away. The air must not be polluted. The waters must be kept clean. Animals must not be hunted down and killed to extinction. Humanity must be free to praise and glorify God by being alive and healthy, both in body and spirit. God must be free to love and care for us as only He knows how to do. He must be able to love us as a true relative — a Father — Ateunyapi, and we must remove within us whatever it is that keeps that love from flowing into us.

It is a tightly-knit system and nothing is ever lost. Even when something or someone dies, it still stays within the family. The flesh returns to the earth and the spirit returns to the Creator. Things change from one place to another, or from one form to another, but they are never destroyed or lost to the family. Water can change to ice or steam, but it's always there. The sun can draw up water but it always returns as rain to the earth. Animals and vegetables can be killed and eaten but they give life to people who are eating them. People can lose their bodies, but their spirits join with God, like relatives returning home after a long journey. They are welcomed home with great joy and feasting.

The Lakota people can be happy because of their tradition which has enriched the church with the wisdom of MITAKUYE OYASIN. It is a wisdom that the world desperately needs to hear — that the entire world and all the people spread across its face, are one family. They are all kinsfolk and when they kill or oppress one group of people, they are killing and oppressing their family members, their relatives. Not only are they killing **them,** they are killing **themselves.** This is not so hard to understand and there is a little bit of local expression that puts it very well: "What goes around, comes around." Since the world is a great web of interdependence, what happens to one, happens to all somehow. Eventually, it sets up a chain-reaction which influences the entire earthly community.

The world which presently lives under the shadow of the atom bomb desperately needs to hear about these words: ALL MY RELATIVES. They are the truth, they are real and they are the same words that Jesus was speaking in another time and place, but for all times and all places. "What you do to the least of my brethren, you do to me," He said. The Lakota people can be glad of their traditional wisdom — as glad as Peter was that day when Jesus said to him: "Blessed are you Simon son of Jonah, for flesh and blood have not revealed this to you, but my Father who is in heaven has revealed this to you."

O Lord, who shall sojourn in your tent? Who shall dwell on your sacred mountain? Psalm 15

God heard the cries and pleading of those Lakota people long ago when they prayed and cried for spiritual guidance. He answered them with the words: "MITAKUYE OYASIN — ALL MY RELATIVES," and they received wisdom and sustenance for their earthly journey.

Today, when Jesus comes among the Lakota people, he hears the words, "All My Relatives," and recognizes them as his own. It is like the Gospel story of the Good Shepherd and the sheep. Jesus said: "I know mine and mine know me." They recognize his voice and He recognizes them when He sees them. One other time, He said: "I have not come to destroy, but to fulfill." Jesus loves and praises the good wherever He finds it, and when there is wisdom and goodness in a tradition such as the Lakota tradition, Jesus praises it and welcomes it. Once He was told by His disciples that someone was casting out evil spirits in His name. Shouldn't we tell them to stop, they asked Jesus? His reply gives us pause to reflect: "Leave them alone, for he who is not against me is for me."

Medicine

Another insight of the Lakota tradition which complements the Gospel message, is the manner in which religion or spirituality is regarded as **medicine.** Often a very spiritual person is called a "medicine man," that is, a person who is able to heal the sufferings of others in the community. He has been given power by the Great Spirit through His spirits to see things that others do not see, to hear things that others do not hear, and to have spiritual healing flow through him for the benefit of those around him and who call for him. If he is humble and truthful, admitting that the power is not from him but only flows through him, then only good happens. If he is proud of the power and abusive of it, wasting it on petty things, no lasting good will come of it and he will be discovered eventually for what he is. He is like the tree in the Gospel story which bears bad fruit. Jesus warned his followers about this kind of spiritual abuse: "By their fruits you will know them," He said.

This belief, that religion is medicine, is completely biblical as well. We find many references to God's healing of the wounds and sinfulness of Israel, His chosen people. In the ministry of Jesus as described in the four Gospels, He is porytrayed as a healer. When John the Baptist sent his own disciples to Jesus asking Him if He was the Messiah, Jesus sent word back that the blind see, the deaf hear, the lame walk and the poor have heard some good news. Yet Jesus came to heal much more than bodily illness. He came to heal the invisible wounds in people's souls. These were the really important diseases, the ones on the inside which were sapping the spiritual energy from the people because of fear and guilt. Jesus came to heal souls and for this reason was born in poverty, suffered like other people in every way that they suffer and eventually was pierced and died on the cross in a pitiful condition. Before He died, He pleaded on behalf of all humanity to God, His Father, asking for forgiveness and healing for even his own persecutors.

The church, from the very beginning of its history, carried on Jesus' work of healing as we see from this portion of scripture:

> "The people carried the sick into the streets and laid them on cots and mattresses so that when Peter passed by at least his shadow might fall on one or another of them. Crowds from the towns around Jerusalem would gather, too, bringing their sick and those who were troubled by unclean spirits, all of whom were healed.   **Acts 5:15-16**

As his legacy then, Jesus left His followers the means of healing their spiritual sickness (and sometimes their bodily sickness also) in seven sacred rituals which we call the sacraments. By means of these sacred actions and their special signs and symbols, the community can experience the power of God flowing into their lives. This power is able to lift them up from their sufferings and mend their broken lives. All of them are healers, each in their own way, touching some aspect of people's lives, but the Eucharist is **the healer.** As the bread is broken, the death of Jesus is relived and the broken community experiences its oneness and its true family relationship at the foot of the cross, as it were, where all are forgiven.

In the following brief overview, it is possible to see how each of the sacraments is a healing process in the midst of the community, applying divine medicine to the illness of humanity. Later, in the last chapter, the Eucharist is discussed again under the aspect of its ability to heal cultural wounds as well.

1. BAPTISM: "The water that I will give will become a fountain of life within you, leaping up to provide eternal life." **John 4: 13-14**
We share in the life of the family of God, coming in to the circle and are no longer alone. We are cleansed of selfishness.

2. CONFIRMATION: "The Spirit whom I will send you will guide you to all truth." **John 16: 13**
We are no longer blind and lost, but have found our way to the light.

3. EUCHARIST: "Those who come to me will never be hungry, those who believe in me will never be thirsty." **John 6: 35**
We have food to nourish us along the way, to strengthen us for our journey.

4. RECONCILIATION: "Let us celebrate because this child of mine who was dead has come back to life." **Luke 15:23**
Our good relations have been restored with God and his family. We have found our way back home, and have been purified again.

5. ANOINTING OF THE SICK: "Jesus stretched out his hand and touched him saying: Be healed." **Mark 1: 41**

We are offered comfort and companionship from our family of God, and hope in God's wisdom and strength.

6. MATRIMONY: "They are no longer two but one."

Matthew 19: 6

We care for one another's needs and the generations to come.

7. ORDINATION: "Come after me and I will make you fishers of men." **Matthew 4: 19**

Our ministers are healers and reconcilers in God's family, restoring it and strengthening it.

The Value of Generosity

Generosity is something that any real Lakota should have and display. The leader or chief of the people ought to display this characteristic virtue to an eminent degree, and by following the example of others, the Lakota people learn to provide for their family members and relatives, as well as the needy ones in the community.

Therefore, a person is looked up to and respected not only for their ability to provide food, clothing and shelter, but also for their ability to give generously and not count the cost.

It is better to give a lot than to have a lot and keep it for yourself, according to the Lakota mentality. In fact, to be called "stingy" is one of the worst insults that can be said of anyone.

When an important occasion comes along, people honor someone in their midst or a dead loved one with a celebration that is called a "giveaway" or "otuhan." During the year previous to this occasion, goods and foods are collected and set aside for the grand day. On the day itself, the donor gives it all away "in honor" of the designated party. Thus, the donor is honored when others receive from his generosity, and the one for whom this is done is also honored, because all of this is done in his/her name. In the old days, this kind of giveaway could reach "fever" proportions when a donor would get carried away and strip himself of everything he owned, to the great admiration of all present. Such display of generosity on behalf of others would so excite the on-lookers, that they would often be inspired to do the same and a great celebration of giving would take place, with great shouting and giving away of belongings.

It is easy to see how this value is completely in harmony with the message of Jesus, who urges His followers: "Go, sell what you have and give to the poor." Perhaps this great value of Lakota generosity has more in common with the early church community which held all things in common than our western European attitude of individual ownership and savings accounts!

Such generosity is only one of the four great cardinal values that the Lakota understand as the underpinning of their way of life. The others are courage, respect and wisdom. They are also qualities that any true Lakota should possess to be worthy of the name.

Earth

For the Lakota people, visiting the hills was similar to the biblical notion of "going up to Jerusalem." It was more than a physical journey from one place to another. It was a spiritual journey as well. **Psalm** 121 says: "I lift up my eyes to the hills. . ." and when many of the Lakota think of the Black Hills, they think in such spiritual terms as these. It is to lift up one's spirit to the Great Spirit who beckons us with such beauty in creation.

As was mentioned earlier, the very earth is sacred to the Lakota people. They are not ashamed to sit on the ground and in fact, sometimes, prefer it, for then they are close to their mother who sustains them and gives them life.

Likewise, in the Christian religion, we also have the belief that we come from the earth. In **Genesis**, we find the story of how God took the dust of the earth and formed it into a living being. The ashes placed on our foreheads on Ash Wednesday are a humbling reminder that we have come from the dust of the earth and are going to return to it one day. We are all children of the Earth our Mother — Lakota and Christian.

Christianity has reflected also on the rocks and stones of its past experience. God has been called upon and sung to as the "Rock of Ages," (and it was on the tablets of stone that God wrote the Ten Commandments). Jesus Christ was born in a small cave in a rocky hillside at Bethlehem and was buried in a hollowed-out rock near Jerusalem. It was the stone that sealed his body within itself for three days, and it was the stone which rolled back to release the resurrected Christ to the light of the day. Jesus had referred to himself as the stone which the builders rejected, but which was used by God.

Therefore, even in the Christian and Jewish religions, the "rock" is a symbol of God. The Psalms in the Bible often talk about God as a "rock" to which people could go for safety from enemies. God protects them like a mighty fort on a hill, or like a cave in a mountainside. Jesus reminded to build ourselves on the "rock" not the sand, so that we wouldn't fall apart when hard times come to test us.

Spirits

For the Lakota, both good and bad spirits are present in the universe and contact with them is possible and occurs frequently.

Strange as this may sound to some people's ears, it is really nothing new to Christianity. Traditional Catholic teaching has admitted the existence of both good and bad angels. (Bad angels are called "devils" of course, the chief of which is Satan.) A guardian angel has been given to each person and other angels adore God and do his bidding continually in heaven. In both the Christian and Lakota traditions, the angel-spirit is a personal helper and a bearer of messages. It was an angel who appeared to Joseph in a dream and warned him to escape with Mary and the child, Jesus, into Egypt. Angels were present in the desert after Jesus' temptation where they were "ministering to Him." In the Psalms, we read: "In the sight of the angels I will sing your praises Lord" **(Psalm 138:1)**. This kind of power is not so far removed from the calling of the spirits to witness the actions of the Lakota holy man and those gathered with him in a sacred ceremony.

If we search the scriptures, we find many passages which teach us about these good spirits who are called "angels."

There are good **spirits** which bring messages to God's people:
"Are they (angels) not all ministering spirits, sent to serve those who are to inherit salvation?"   **Hebrews 1: 14**

There are spirits who are the **Four Winds:**
"He makes the winds his messengers."   **Psalm 104: 4**

. . .and the striking passage from **Zechariah 6:5:**
"These are the four winds of the heavens coming forth after being reviewed by the Lord of all the earth. . ."

Lakota Christians would not be surprised to learn that there are both good and evil spirits, and that we need to discern between the two and assess their influence in our lives. Traditionally, Christ and the saints had to deal with angels and devils, as we call them, and determine whether or not they would accept their assistance. Whatever we call them, there are influences and powers for good and for evil in each of our lives, and we need to turn to the Spirit for the gift of discernment to decide what is a good power or an evil power.

Opening the Scriptures

On the road to Emmaus, Jesus walked along with his disciples and as it says in **Luke 24:**

"He interpreted for them every passage of scripture which referred to him."

We, too, can search the scriptures for the wonderful ways in which God calls forth our traditions and cultural ways of speaking and doing.

There are many themes in scripture which are completely at home in the Lakota tradition.

Sometimes, these words and phrases which have **symbolic** meaning for the Lakota people leap out at the reader. At other times, it is necessary to search them out.

There are many examples of these common symbols:

Eagles
Exodus 19:4
Psalm 103:5
Isaiah 40:31
Deuteronomy 28:49 and 32:11
Jeremiah 48:40, 14:16
Ezekiel 1:10, 10:14, 17:3
Revelation 4:7, 12:14

Lightning
Psalm 144:6
Matthew 24:27
Luke 17: 24
Luke 10:18
Job 37: 3
Exodus 19: 16, 20:18

Psalm 77: 18, 97: 4, 135:7
Revelation 4: 5, 8:5, 11:19

Earth
Exodus 9: 29, 19: 5
*Deuteronomy 10:14
Psalm 24:1
I Corinthians 10:26
Exodus 20:24
Job 5:25
Deuteronomy 32: 1
Job 38:4
Psalm 33: 5
Psalm 65: 9
Psalm 67: 6
Ezekiel 34: 27

Numbers 14: 21
Ecclesiastes 12: 7
Psalm 77: 18
Psalm 97: 1
Ecclesiastes 1: 4
Isaiah 40: 22 and 28
   45: 22
   66: 1
Ezekiel 43: 2
Hosea 2: 22
Habakuk 2: 14, 3: 3 and 9
Matthew 5: 5, 35
Mark 4: 28
Psalm 148: 7
Psalm 85: 11
Job 28: 5
Psalm 146: 4

Directions (Four)
Matthew 2: 1
Revelations 21: 13
Psalm 103: 12
Psalm 107: 3
Zechariah 8: 7
I Chronicles 9: 23-24
Psalm 89: 12
Isaiah 43: 6
Psalm 139: 9-10
*Zechariah 6: 5

Sun
Psalm 84: 12
Psalm 89: 37

Matthew 5: 45
   13: 43
   17: 2
Revelations 1:16, 10: 1

Sky
Job 37: 18
Deuteronomy 33: 26
Psalm 18: 11
Isaiah 45: 8

Rock
Psalm 18: 1-3, 33-34
Deuteronomy 32: 4, 18
Psalm 92: 15, Psalm 28: 1
Genesis 28: 18, 22

Good Spirits
Numbers 16: 22
   27: 16
Psalm 104: 4
*Zecariah 6: 5
I John 4: 1
Matthew 4: 11

Mountains (Sacred)
Ezekiel 20: 40-44
Exodus 18: 5, 19: 16, 31: 18
Exodus 4: 27
Matthew 5: 1, 14: 23, 15: 29
   4: 8, 17: 1
Luke 4: 5
Mark 9: 2
Revelations 21: 10

Flute
Matthew 11: 17
Luke 7: 32
I Kings 1: 40
Psalm 150: 4

Incense
Psalm 141: 2
Leviticus 16: 13

Pity/Humility
Psalm 67: 1-2, Psalm 25
Sirach 3: 17-28

Name
Acts 4: 12
Philemon 2: 9

National Calamity
Psalm 74
Psalm 80: 4-7

Hospitality
Leviticus 19: 33-34

Tree
Genesis 2: 9
Ezekiel 47: 12
Ezekiel 17: 24
Acts 5: 29-32
Galatians 3: 13
Jeremiah 17: 7-8

Mark 4: 30-33
Matthew 13: 30-32

Dreams
Genesis 28: 10-19
Genesis 31: 24
Genesis 37: 5
Numbers 12: 6
I Kings 3: 5
Job 33: 15
Daniel 2: 4, 36
Matthew 1: 20
        2: 13, 19
        2: 12, 22
        27: 19
Joel 2: 28
Acts 2: 17
Daniel 1: 17

Generosity
Sirach 3: 29-30   Matthew 10:8
        4: 1-10   John 3: 51
Acts 20: 35
Luke 6: 38
Matthew 5: 42
Luke 9: 10-17

Morning Star
Revelations 2: 28
            22: 16
Matthew 2: 2

Circle
Isaiah 40: 22

Offerings/Vows
Psalm 56: 12   Jonah 2: 10
Psalm 50: 14   Genesis 28: 20-22
Psalm 66: 13-15
Exodus 32: 6

Cleansing
Psalm 51: 7
James 4: 7-11
Isaiah 1: 16-18
Ezekiel 36: 25-28
Psalm 51: 10, 7
2 Corinthians 7: 1

Vision Quest
Psalm 25: 4-5
Psalm 88: 1-2, 10
Psalm 69: 4-5   Sirach 2:1-18
Psalm 70: 6   Isaiah 41:17-20
Psalm 71: 20
Psalm 77: 1-10
Jonah 3: 5-11

Spirit
Psalm 90: 2
Psalm 139: 7-10
Psalm 104: 30
Isaiah 61: 1
Luke 4: 18
Matthew 4: 1, 12: 28
John 4: 24
Mark 1: 10
Genesis 1: 2

John 3: 5

Reverence/Respect
Psalm 89: 6-9
Hebrews 12: 28
Matthew 21: 37
Mark 12: 6
Luke 20: 13
Leviticus 19: 32
Ephesians 5: 33
2 Chronicles 19: 6-7
Sirach 3: 1-16

Wisdom
Psalm 51: 6   Sirach 4: 11-19
Psalm 37: 30
Psalm 90: 12
Proverbs 3: 13
          10: 31
Luke 2: 40, 52
Ecclesiastes 1: 1-29
Colossians 1: 9

Life After Death
Psalm 56: 13

Fasting
Matthew 6: 16, and 4: 2
Joel 1: 14   1 Corinthians 7: 5
Psalms 35: 13, 69:10, 109: 24

Sacrifice
Psalm 51: 17   Psalm 50: 1-6

Ezra 4: 2

Psalm 54: 6

   107: 22

Psalm 107: 22

Hebrews 13: 16, 10: 12

I Peter 2: 5

Courage

Psalm 27: 14

Psalm 56: 11

Psalm 31: 24

Isaiah 41:10

Romans 12: 1

Psalm 69: 30-34

Dawn

Psalm 143: 7-8

Psalm 5

Way

Psalm 5: 8   Psalm 67: 3

   27: 11

   119:37, 9-16

Isaiah 57: 10

N.B. Sirach = Ecclesiastes

*Denotes Remarkable Commonality

Chapter 5

All Things in Christ

"God has given us to understand the mystery, namely his plan to bring all things in the heavens and on earth into one under Christ's headship."   **Ephesians 1: 9-10**

Another method of adapting the Gospel message to another tradition was used during the Patristic era. The teachers of the early Church engaged in a process of reflecting on and calling into service of Christ the signs and customs of pre-Christian tradition. Many of these signs and customs were understood by them as **types** or **prefigures** of Christ and His message.

The entire Old Testament as non-Christian literature was brought into this process of reflection and service of Christ. Perhaps this seemed an inevitable thing to do for the Fathers, since the apostles themselves had done exactly the same thing.

Peter, in his first letter, writes about the flood and how the ark saved those who were in it from drowning while water and darkness covered the earth. He likens baptism to this story:

> That water is a type of the baptism which saves you now, and which is not the washing of physical dirt but a pledge made to God. . .   **I Peter 3: 20-21**

The Fathers saw in the events and people of Israel's history the foreshadowings of Christ. The saving blood of the lamb on the doorposts of the Israelites was a prefigure of the saving blood of Christ on the wood of the cross; the serpent lifted up in the desert to heal the Israelites was a prefigure of Christ lifted up on the cross; Moses the lawgiver of Sinai was a prefigure of Christ on the mount of the Beatitudes giving the new law.

St. Paul seems to have employed this very same process when he "reworked" the ritual meal of the Passover which took place on the night before Jesus died:

"Christ our passover has been sacrificed."

I Corinthians 5: 7

Just as the lamb was slain and its ultimate sacrifice — its shedding of blood — saved the Israelites on their journey out of the slavery of Egypt, so did Christ's broken body and His bloodshed deliver the people who believed in Him. He brought them out of the slavery of paralyzing guilt and deadly fear.

As the Fathers understood it, once the event of Jesus had taken place in the history of humanity, nothing was viewed in the same way again. The Passover of the Israelites was no longer just the Passover — it was transformed and given new meaning because it now prepared them for the event of Christ. This transformation was also known as recapitulation, a theme developed in particular by St. Irenaeus in his works, **Against Heresy** and **Proof of the Apostolic Preaching.**

Irenaeus compared Adam to Christ, since Adam was formed from the earth while it was virginal soil, having been untilled. Christ, too, was born of a virgin. Eve and Mary were compared negatively, since Eve disobeyed God and brought suffering to humanity, while Mary obeyed God and brought salvation. Eve gave physical life as mother of the human race, while Mary was regarded as the mother of the new people of God since she gave birth to the Savior. The tree of knowledge brought about the fall and the tree of the cross regained eternal life for humanity.

When Irenaeus reflected on Moses, he saw in him a type of Christ who gave the people a law, and deliverance from their captors in Egypt by passing through the waters of the Red Sea, eventually leading them to the promised land. As he said:

For in these things our affairs were being rehearsed, the

-118-

word of God at that time prefiguring what was to be. But now, bringing us out of the bitter servitude He has caused to gush forth in abundance in the desert a stream of water from a rock — the rock is Himself. He, too, frees us by stretching forth his hands and takes us and bears us into the kingdom of the Father. **(#46 Proof)**

For some people today, this idea may prove very helpful and they may wish to apply this process to the Lakota culture. Perhaps one of the greatest prefigures of Christ is the Sacred Pipe. Just as the Pipe is a means of unity between humanity and God, so is Christ a mediator in his own body and spirit. Just as the Pipe is material and spiritual, so is Christ human and divine. Just as the Pipe was brought by a woman, so is Christ given to us through a woman — Mary. Just as a new moral code is given with the gift of the Pipe, so is the new law given to humanity with the message of Christ. The Sacred Pipe woman taught love for all of one's relatives, while Christ taught love for all as relatives — even one's enemies. Just as Mary brought us the "Prince of Peace" in Jesus, her son, the sacred woman brought the Sacred Pipe of peace to the people.

The buffalo (Tatanka) may also be seen as a "type" of Christ since Jesus had said of Himself that others "ate his flesh," they would "have life." Therefore we may see in the buffalo and its symbol as the buffalo skull, a figure of the Lord himself. He also, in a more perfect way, gave himself as a sacrifice for the people. In the Eucharist, He gives himself as their food to nourish and sustain them in their every need, providing for them so that "they lack nothing." He, too, is a true "relative," making life possible for all.

Yutapi Wakan. . .They are eating holy.

The Cross and the Sacred Tree

Sometimes, as we have said, there are areas in the Christian and Lakota spiritual traditions which complement each other. There are also instances where something in the Lakota tradition may be a "type." This makes it possible for Christians who are Lakota to participate fully in their traditional Lakota ceremonies, while seeing the spirit of Christ present in them as well. This section tries to give examples of how the Sundance ceremony and tree can be re-oriented as "types" of the passion of Christ.

There seem to be many parallels between what happens during the ceremony of the Sundance and the passion of Jesus. When the entire group assembles in the woods to cut down the tree, it is a young tree in its prime that is singled out and cut down. Jesus was a young man in his prime when he was "cut down" by his enemies. Just as Jesus was taken by his enemies in a grove of trees, so is this sacred tree taken by "enemies," for the people go out to get it as if going toward a hostile nation. Once Jesus is captured, he is stripped and when the tree is cut down, it is stripped of all its branches except a few at the very top. These branches are given away to the bystanders just as the clothes of Jesus were given away to others standing around. Then the tree is carried in procession to the place where the ceremony will take place and it is set up in a hole dug for it. Jesus, too, carried his cross in a procession to the place where it was placed in a hole in the earth. In both the Sundance and the crucifixion, it is the earth which holds up the "sacred tree." Both the Sundance pole and the cross are called "trees" and it is the apostle Peter who speaks of the cross in this way.

> He was bearing our faults in his own body on the tree so that we might die to our faults and live for holiness. Through his wounds you have been healed.   (I Peter 2:24)

Jesus suffered so that others might be healed and the Sundancer too prays and dances "that the people might live!" Jesus was suspended on the cross for everyone to see and the Sundancer is suspended from the tree as everyone looks on and watches. During the long hot day when Jesus suffered, a man came up and tried to get Jesus to drink something but he turned his head and would not drink. Likewise a tempter enters the circle with a bowl of water and tries to get the dancers to drink, but they are faithful and do not drink. Not far from the cross stood the friends and relatives of Jesus praying with Him, and around the circle stand the friends and relatives of the dancer who watch and encourage him with their prayers.

The Sundancer has his flesh pierced through with a skewer while the hands and feet of Jesus are pierced through with nails. In the end, Jesus was released from the cross after He spoke His dying words: "It is finished!" and the Sundancer breaks away from the sacred tree when his prayer for the people is finished.

When the crucifixion was completed, the body of Jesus was placed on the earth and cared for by his relatives and friends. Once the Sundance is over, the dancers lie on the earth and receive care from the others. When the dancers are refreshed and renewed, they rise up and return to be with their people. Likewise, once Christ rises up from within the earth, he rejoins his people in a new way, a spiritual way to care for them to this very day.

These are some of the parallels that may appear as one watches and reflects on the ceremony of the Sundance. There are some internal spiritual parallels that are possible, too, between Christ and the Sundancer. Such as the following: **courage** to suffer "long and hard" on behalf of others, a vision which sees the life and health of the people as more important than one's self; a spirit of **sacrifice** which is willing to suffer for others and before God; and finally **humility** or brokenness of spirit as the proper stance that one must take before the Creator and Spirit of all life. Both Christ and the Sundancer appear "pitiful" before God who holds the meaning of all things, as they plead for others.

-122-

If you can have some share in the sufferings of Christ be glad.
I Peter 4: 13

In all of these parallels, however, it is important to understand that the passion of Jesus is not identical to the suffering of the Sundancer. Each has its own place, and perhaps this is where the Christian begins to take a deeper look at things before him as he participates in the traditional religious ceremony. Scripture tells us that Jesus sacrificed "once and for all." This means that it was His unique role as the Son of God to suffer in order to save the entire world throughout all of history. The accomplishment of Jesus does not make the Sundance devoid of meaning but complements it. Another way of putting this is that a Christian Lakota person who takes part in the Sundance does so with an added dimension. When he steps into the sacred circle, he also steps into the passion of Jesus as well. Jesus said once: "I have not come to destroy the old, but to fulfill it" and so with this in mind, the Lakota Christian suffers and intercedes for the people in company with Christ. He can say to himself: "I am doing this with Jesus, I have in mind to offer my prayers and sufferings in the way that Jesus did. I am modeling myself after him and all the others who have gone before me, piercing their flesh and shedding their blood for their relations, for their health, to renew their hopes and dreams, for peace between all races" and whatever else comes to mind.

As the Sundancer and the people around him look up to the tree standing at the center of the circle, they can also see the cross in and through this tree. They are "overlayed," one on the other, for one who looks with this kind of spiritual vision. If anyone reflects on a tree and studies how it is doing things in nature, they will find out that it is like a tube which takes things like water and nourishment up through itself into its outer-most leaves. It also takes sunlight and air into its top-most parts and brings these down through itself into the earth below where it spreads out more roots. In this way, life passes up and down through the tree and earth and sky are exchanged. Spiritually, by means of the sacred tree of life and the cross, heaven comes down to earth and earth reaches up to heaven. Prayers go up and help comes down, for the betterment of all the people.

"Just as Moses lifted up the serpent in the wilderness, so the Son of Man must be lifted up, so that whoever believes in Him may not perish but have eternal life."

John 3:14

When reflecting on the Lakota Christian's participation in the Sundance, it is possible to see how this carries out in a way that is special to the Lakota culture, a challenge that St. Paul gives every Christian. He says that we are to "fill up what is lacking in the sufferings of Christ." Each generation of Christians can extend the meaning of the cross into their time and place on behalf of those with whom they live: their family and friends; their immediate communities and the wider community of the world. They show by their own suffering that the individual must never think that he is the center of everything, but must show how generosity and unselfishness are the only way that the world can continue. It is the vocation of every Christian to copy Christ's becoming flesh, by putting some flesh on the words of the Gospel. Being willing to suffer and do hard things for the people is at the heart of Christianity and it is at the heart of the Sundance as well. These two great traditions come together to complement each other, they do not cancel each other. Each is a form of sacrifice:

"My sacrifice is a humble spirit, O God, you will not reject a humble and contrite heart!"   **Psalm 51**

A passage in **I Peter** seems to come very close to the sentiments of Lakota Christians participating in the Sundance:

God will bless you for this if you endure the pain of undeserved suffering because you are conscious of his will. For what credit is there if you endure suffering you deserve for doing something wrong? But if you endure suffering even when you have done right, God will bless you for it. Christ

-125-

himself suffered for you and left you an example, so that you would follow in his steps. (I Peter 2: 19-22)

The Lakota people and the Sundancers see their bodies as instruments of prayer and sacrifice, as one old Lakota man said:

A man's body is his own, and when he gives his body or his flesh, he is giving the only thing which really belongs to him. We know that all creatures on the earth were placed here by Wakantanka. Thus, if a man says he will give a horse to Wakantanka, he is only giving to Wakantanka that which already belongs to him. I might give tobacco or other articles in the Sundance, but if I give these and kept back the best no one would believe that I was in earnest. I must give something that I really value to show that my whole being goes with the lesser gifts; therefore I promise to give my body.
(Chased by Bears, **Teton Sioux Music,** Densmore Bureau of American Ethnology, Bulletin 61: p. 96).

It is a short trip for the Christian Lakota to make from this traditional attitude to the attitude of which St. Paul speaks when he encourages his fellow Christians to have the "mind of Christ" and to "put on Christ" and model themselves after him. St. Francis of Assisi tried constantly to model himself after the pattern shown to him on the hill of Calvary, and it is a well-known tradition that he received wounds in his hands and feet similar to the wounds of Christ. Those non-Indian critics who feel repulsed by the "unnecessary suffering" of the Sundance might benefit from recalling how Christians honor the stigmata of St. Francis of Assisi and how acceptable this unnecessary suffering is in western mentality as well.

If the Sundance gives the participant an opportunity to reflect on the value of sacrifice on behalf of the people, how much more can a Christian Lakota participate in the same ritual emphasizing further the sufferings of Christ in his own mind and heart? Again, it is important to remember that the Lakota Christian participant does not give up the Lakota heritage but participates that much more!

"I have not come to destroy but to fulfill." **Matthew 13:52**

Chapter 6

A Lakota Liturgy

The Eucharist is a sacred meal and it is also a family meal. It is sacred because it is no ordinary meal. It is a spiritual meal — with a table that is set by God our Father with special food which nourishes us and provides us with spiritual healing. It is no secret that we are a broken people living in a broken world. It is this family meal which expresses our true and deep relationship — our kinship — with God the Father and our human family. When we gather around his table, we are all relatives. We belong to Him and one another, and we look to one another for support and encouragement. In this way, we build up the community which has been damaged and stands in need of healing. Therefore, we depend on one another for forgiveness of our shortcomings and mistakes. We come together to ask forgiveness if we have failed, or to forgive freely and generously if we have been hurt by others. What better place than the liturgy then, to heal the cultural hurts that have been inflicted upon others even during this sacred family meal!

By forgiving each other and overcoming our mistakes, we learn to grow together and respect each other. We are like a family that is on a journey together toward fulfillment of our deepest yearnings for happiness and peace. We are all trying to grow up to be like our brother, Jesus, who suffered and died for each of us, and who teaches us to respect the dignity and identity of everyone we meet along His way. We come together out of a need to be with others and to express ourselves according to our own culture, because that is the way we have been made by the Creator. "It is not good for man to live alone" also means that we are made for community and family living and are part of our God-given culture.

"This is what I pray, kneeling before the Father from whom every family whether spiritual or natural takes its name — may He give you the power to grow strong, to grasp the breadth, length, heighth and depth, until you are filled with the utter fullness of God." **(Ephesians 3)**

The Bishops of the United States have made it very clear that they wish to see efforts at preaching the Gospel and incorporating culture into worship among Native Americans that will respect their dignity and leave their identity as native peoples intact. Their **Statement on American Indians** of May 4, 1977, was an effort at reconciliation for past failures to respect Native American culture and an encouragement to take up the task of adapting programs and liturgies to Native American culture in the local churches:

The Christian faith should celebrate and strengthen the many diverse cultures which are the product of human hope and aspiration. The Gospel message must take root and grow within each culture and each community. Faith finds expression in and through the particular values, customs and institutions of the people who hear it. It seeks to take flesh in each culture, within each nation, within each race. . .
Statement of U.S. Catholic Bishops on American Indians, p. 3.

What follows in the next few pages is an example of how some adaptations in the liturgy have been made in one particular community composed predominantly of Native American children — an Indian school. The main portion of this group are children between the ages of six and fifteen years old who live at St. Joseph's Indian School for nine months out of the year. Their reservation homes are located in both North and South Dakota. A survey confirmed their desire to have a "Lakota Mass."

-129-

Survey of the Childrens' Attitude on Worship

The children who were in the upper grades (from level four to eight) were given a question to consider concerning worship in the school chapel and then the answers were collected. There were many responses, in fact, every child responded but only a sampling is given here. Their answers and reflections are unselfconscious and expressive of the way in which they feel about how things "ought to be" and how much they appreciate their own spirituality and tradition.

The question they were asked is as follows: "Do you feel that God likes to have Indian things in church?" Some of their answers are given here for our reflection, according to grade level.

Grade Four: Yes, because we are Indian and we are still praying to Him.

Grade Five: Yes, because all of us are human and he loves every kind of human like Indian, white, black and yellow.

Yes, because God loves everyone and would like to have many different kinds of people in his house.

Grade Six: Yes, because God is not prejudiced and He likes all people, and everybody likes God.

Grade Seven: Yes, because we just have it the same way but with our own kind of culture.

Yes, because He came for everybody on earth, and could just as well have been born an Indian.

Grade Eight: Yes, because every color of people are brothers and sisters now.

Yes, because God likes people to be who they are and not prove themselves to others. He likes people to appreciate themselves and their good ways of doing things. We need, and especially the young kids, to start getting acquainted with Indian ways so later in life, they can be proud they are Indian, so if a white person calls them down they won't regret being Indian because if they do, they might do something to harm themselves. . .

The Lakota Mass

What follows is an example of the liturgy as it has been celebrated at St. Joseph's Indian School, incorporating elements of the Lakota culture and spirituality.

It is a celebration of the Feast of Christ the King and may be adapted as the "Feast of Christ Our Chief."

It is important to realize that the cultural contributions to the liturgy which have been incorporated are not taking the place of or removing anything that is essential to the Eucharistic celebration. They are additions to it and are examples of what might be called the principle of **illustration.** They add to, and do not subtract from the liturgy. Candles and white garments add to and further illustrate the meaning of the Rite of Baptism. The essence of which is the pouring of the water and the words: "I baptize you in the name of the Father, the Son, and the Holy Spirit." Likewise, in this liturgy, the reading from Black Elk further illustrates or supports the readings from the Bible, and the four colored cloths in the sanctuary illustrate further the unity of all creation both in heaven and on earth around the table of the Lord. The Eucharistic words: "Do this in memory of Me," remain the same, but now it is the Lakota people who are doing the remembering, not the Romans, or the Germans, or the Irish. The Lakota may remember and celebrate in their own way, to the greater honor and glory of God who is the Father of all nations.

"He will wipe away the tears from all faces and take away
forever all insults and mockery against his land and people."
Jesus Itancan — Jesus our Chief

Feast of Christ Our Chief

Theme:
In today's Gospel, Jesus tells a story about a great chief who wanted to honor his own son's wedding, so he prepared a feast and invited some guests. They were not willing to come so he invited everyone to come no matter who they were. Like the great chief, God wants to be generous to us, but we don't always accept His gifts and His food. This Mass is His meal so let us accept the honor and gather around.

Opening Song:
The "Flag Song" is song by which we honor God, our Grandfather. The entrance procession is made up of the Cross bearer, Lakota staff bearer, four dancers carrying the four sacred colors (black, red, yellow, white) and one dancer carrying the Sacred Pipe.

Purification Rite

Invocation:
O God You are the Great Spirit, and You are present everywhere in the world! We turn to You in the West, and praise You. In your wisdom You send us your creature water.
To it, You have given many powers:
  —the power to cleanse and heal,
  —the power to make things grow,
  and the power to satisfy the thirst of all the creatures on the earth.

Baptismal Renewal: Therefore, your Son Jesus chose this creature water as a means of joining him in his sacred way.
Through water poured over us at Baptism we became relatives of one family under the same Spirit.
And now we want to make new our promise to follow Him on His sacred way for we have not followed Him as we should.
Pour out your Spirit over us again and renew the face of the earth!
Cleanse us from evil
and heal our wounds.
Once again we will live
if we drink of your living water.

Aspersion: (With these words ended, the celebrant sprinkles the people with the cedar branch dipped in water.)

Penance Rite: Jesus You have sacrificed yourself for all the people, (Lord have mercy). Itancan waonsila ye.
Jesus, the people look up to you, (Christ have mercy). Christ waonsila ye.
Jesus, all nations come to you, (Lord have mercy). Itancan waonsila ye.

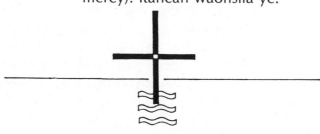

Opening Prayer:　　O God our Father and Great Spirit, you have called us to honor your Son in this feast of sacred food and drink. We are honored also by your invitation and we wish to bring the gift of ourselves to You in joy. Grant this through Christ our Lord. R. Amen.

Lakota Reading:　　Black Elk's version of unity and peace.

Reader:　　"Listen to these words of Black Elk:"

Reading:　　"Against the (holy) tree there was a man standing with arms held wide in front of him. I looked hard at him, and I could not tell what people he came from. He was not a Wasichu and he was not an Indian. His hair was long and hanging loose, and on the left side of his head he wore an eagle feather. His body was strong and good to see, and it was painted red. I tried to recognize him, but I could not make him out. He was a very fine-looking man. While I was staring hard at him, his body began to change and became very beautiful with all colors of light and around him there was light. He spoke like singing: "My life is such that all earthly beings and growing things belong to me. Your father, the Great Spirit, has said this. You, too, must say this."
—**Black Elk Speaks,** p. 208

(Non-scriptural readings may be introduced sometimes prior to the scripture readings. Hence, this provides an excellent opportunity to draw on the wealth of many great speakers and storytellers of the past.)

Scripture Reading: **Isaiah 25: 6-10**

On this mountain the Lord of hosts will provide for all peoples a feast of rich foods and choice drink, juicy, rich food and pure, choice drink.

On this mountain He will remove the cloud of gloom, the shroud of death that hangs over the earth.

He will swallow up death forever. The Lord God will wipe away the tears from all faces and take away forever all insults and mockery against his land and people. The Lord has spoken!

Response: "I shall live in the lodge of the Great Spirit all the days of my life."

Psalm 23: (Adapted)

The Great Spirit is my chief, He takes care of all my needs.

He leads me to restful waters and refreshes my spirit.

R.

He guides me along a good path, and even though I walk through darkness, my heart is brave because He is with me.

R.

He spreads out a feast for me and puts my enemies to shame. He anoints my head and I have many good things because of Him.

R.

Psalm Alleluia:

Sweet grass, cedar or tobacco is burned as all prepare to hear the Gospel reading.

The Gospel: Matthew 22: 1-10

Jesus told several other stories to show what the Kingdom of Heaven is like. "For instance," He said, "it is like the story of a king who prepared a great wedding feast for his son.

Many guests were invited, and when the feast was ready, he sent messengers to notify everyone that it was time to come. But everyone refused to come.

So he sent other servants to tell them "Everything is ready and the calves have been killed. Come to the wedding!"

But the guests he had invited merely laughed and went on about their business, one to his farm, another to his store. Others beat up his messengers and treated them shamefully, even killing some of them.

Then the angry king sent out his army and destroyed the murderers and burned their city.

And he said to his servants, "The wedding feast is ready, and the guests I invited aren't worthy of the honor.

Now go out to the main roads and invite everyone you see.

So the servants did, and brought in all they could find, good and bad alike, and the feast was filled with guests.

Only goodness and kindness follow me all the days of my life and I shall stay in the lodge of this Great Spirit for years to come.

R.

Homily:	**The Chief gives a feast.**
	The Lakota know what it is to have a great feast in honor of someone. This is something that is deeply embedded in their culture to this day. It is an honor to give gifts and food in a generous manner. If people know how to give and are honored when their gifts are accepted, how much more is this true of God the Father who wishes to give generously to his people. We honor him greatly by accepting his invitation to join his feast of unity at the Eucharistic table in honor of Jesus.
Offertory and Procession:	Bread and wine are brought to the altar by students dressed in native costumes.

*Mini Wiconi

(Water of Life)

Mini Wiconi kin he yukan,
  Ota, ota, ota.
Mini Wiconi kin he yukan,
  Tona waste kin tawa.
Mini etanhan yatkan qani,
  Ota, ota, ota.
Mini etanhan yatkan qa ni,
  Tona waste kilaka.

General Translation:

He has the water of life,
so much of it!
He has the water of life,
whoever is good, it is theirs.
Come and drink from this water,
so much of it!
Come and drink from this water,
whoever wants to.

Eucharistic Prayer for Children I

The **Eucharistic Prayer for Children** is used
and it contains many themes common to
Lakota spirituality.

God our Father,
you have brought us here together
so that we can give you thanks and praise
for all the wonderful things you have done.

We thank you for all that is beautiful in the world
and for the happiness you have given us.
We praise you for daylight
and for your word which lights up our minds.
We praise you for the earth
and all the people who live on it,
and for our life which comes from you.

We know that you are good.
You love us and do great things for us.

Father,
you are always thinking about your people;
you never forget us.
You sent us your Son Jesus,
who gave his life for us
and who came to save us.
He cured sick people;
he cared for those who were poor
and wept with those who were sad.
He forgave sinners
and taught us to forgive each other.
He loved everyone

and showed us how to be kind.
He took children in his arms and blessed them.

God our Father,
all over the world your people praise you.
So now we pray with the whole Church:
with N., our pope and N., our bishop.
In heaven the blessed Virgin Mary,
the apostles and all the saints
always sing your praise.
Now we join with them and with the angels
to adore you.

Father,
because you love us,
you invite us to come to your table.
Fill us with the joy of the Holy Spirit
as we receive the body and blood of your Son.

Lord,
you never forget any of your children.
We ask you to take care of those we love,
especially of N. and N.
and we pray for those who have died.

Remember everyone who is suffering from pain or sorrow.
Remember Christians everywhere
and all other people in the world.

We are filled with wonder and praise
when we see what you do for us
through Jesus your Son.

Lakota Our Father

Prayed by all in Lakota.

Ateunyanpi, mahpiya ekta nanke cin,
nicaje wakanlapi ni; nitokiconze u ni;
mahpiya ekta tokel nitawacin econpi kin
iyecel maka akanl econpi ni.
Anpetu kin otoiyohi aguyapi kin anpetu
kin le el unkupi ye;
na waunhtanipi kin unkakiciktonjapi ye,
unkis tona sicaya ecaunkiconpi kin iyecel
awicaunkiciktonjapi;
na taku wawiyutan un kin el unkayapi sni ye,
tka taku sice kin etanhan eunglakupi ye.
Amen.

Communion:

Yutapi Wakan

Yutapi wakan he niye,
Heon oyate wicani,
Wowastelake kin gluha,
wakanyan lel nanihmapi.

Jesus teunkilapi kin,
Nagi niunkiyapi cin,
Heon wotekiya ktepi,
Eshash wopila wanice.

''Yutapi Wakan'' (Holy Food)
Translation:
Behold, this is holy food!
Because of it the people live.
It is a mystery of love.
Jesus, you suffered on account of me.
Your heart was pierced and emptied,
there is nothing greater than this!

Prayer After Communion:

O Great Spirit, our Father! You have given us this sacred food to nourish us in memory of your Son. We are honored by this great gift and with the help of this food we will live along His holy path for as long as we live until we rejoin you at the heavenly banquet. We ask this through Jesus our Lord, Amen.

Blessing: While the following blessing is being pronounced over the people, the priest holds an eagle feather in his right hand extended over the congregation, saying:

May the Great Spirit
watch over your hearts
that you keep them pure,

Guide your footsteps
that you do not fall,

Reward your spirits
with all good things
both now and hereafter.

Amen.

We have honored Christ our brother and chief. All my relatives, go in peace!

Thanks be to God!

Closing Music: ''Round Dance'' or some other celebrational song accompanies the priest, servers and dancers who carry the Lakota staff, four flags and pipe, on their way out of the church.

Some General Comments on the Liturgy:

1. The Theme: The image of the Good Shepherd who takes care of his people and the Great Chief who cares generously for those in his camp are inter-twined. The symbol of the meal is also present. It is the celebration of unity, peace and brotherhood as well as the means of honoring the "Son" Jesus.

2. Lakota Reading: Black Elk's vision of the beautiful man with arms stretched wide, stands for the place of Jesus in all creation, a place given him by His Father. From this we understand.
Jesus as our Great Leader whom we follow and who calls us to peace and unity.

3. Opening Song: The "Flag Song" is meant in this instance to honor the Great Father, Tunkashila who is God, the Grandfather.

4. Opening Prayer: Adapted to continue the theme of feast and honoring.

5. First Reading: Isaiah's reading is reminiscent of the message of Jesus on another mountain in another time.

6. Response and Psalm: The wording has been adapted to the easily recognizable Lakota way of expressing things.

7. Allelulia and Incense: While the Allelulia is being sung, the priest or deacon may place some grains of cedar, tobacco or sweet grass on a charcoal or wave a braid of sweet grass over the book.

8. Gospel: The story of the desire of a father to honor his son with a feast is easily adapted to Lakota mentality.

9. Offertory Procession: Students are dressed in Lakota costumes and the song is taken from one of the old hymnals translated and composed at the turn of the century in the Dakotas.

10. Eucharistic Prayer: The **Eucharistic Prayer for Children I** is used for the Lakota liturgy and its vocabulary and themes are very appropriate for the traditional spirituality of the Lakota. God is addressed as the Father who brings together all creation present in the worship service. Thanks and praise is given for all the wonderful things God has done, especially the beautiful world and the happi-

ness in the hearts of people. Praise is given for daylight, for the earth (the mother of all) and the people who live on it. God is a true, generous father who loves his children and does "great things" for them. He is "always thinking about" his people. It is the honor of God as a great Chief to be among the people, not isolated from their needs. Especially the poor and the sick were taken care of in olden times, and so it is with the family of God. After the consecration of the bread and wine (it is the Spirit who does this "making holy") the Father invites everyone to come to his table and be filled. All are gathered around his table as a family — as relatives. The vision of this meal becomes wider spiritually as even the dead are remembered and "all other people in the world" are included as well.

As a further adaptation, the word "Father" in the Eucharistic prayer may be substituted by the Lakota "Ateunypi" (Our Father), "Ateyapi" (Father), "Tunkashila" (Grandfather). Therefore, the prayer might begin as follows: "God our Father. . .Wakantanka Ateunyapi" or "God our Father, you are most holy. . .Wakantanka, Ateunyapi you are lila wakan."

11. Our Father: Said together in Lakota.

12. Communion: "Yutapi Wakan" literally means "they are eating holy" and speaks more of action than of a static object to be revered. Thus the Lakota words again taken from one of the old hymnals, are closer to contemporary Eucharistic theology of breaking, eating and uniting.

13. Prayer After Communion: This prayer is also reworded to give more of a sense of Lakota mentality about gift-giving, honoring and food for the journey.

14. Final Blessing: It ends with the reference to everyone as "relatives" which sounds familiar to Lakota ears since the words "Mitakuye Oyasin" (All My Relatives) are commonly used at spiritual meetings and rituals to remind us of our spiritual unity with all creation as relatives. All things are one according to this phrase and it is close to the meaning of the doctrine of the Mystical Body. We have

all shared in the one bread — we are one body and Christ is our head.

15. Closing Song and Procession: The procession is led by the cross, then the Lakota staff which represents the people, as they present themselves to God.

The music is festive since everyone has been fed and received the gift of peace.

The Lakota Staff

The staff is carried in by one of the servers or dancers at the beginning of the service and is placed in the sanctuary where all can see it. It has been decorated with the things that have meaning for the people and that represent them. It is carried in at the beginning to show that the people are giving themselves to God. It says: "We the people are coming to worship the Great Spirit and we give ourselves to Him — all that we are and all that we have we owe to Him."

The staff is decorated with cloths of the four colors of the Four Directions: black, red, yellow and white. It also is wrapped completely around with fur. Some say that this stands for the people being gathered around it.

There are also some eagle feathers hanging from the staff and stand for the desire of the people to receive the blessings of God on themselves and all their relatives. God is represented by these eagle feathers since He is the highest and the greatest. All creatures look to Him for what they need to stay alive and all life and power come from Him.

Altar Decoration:

The altar is draped across the front with a blanket called a ''Chief's Blanket'' which is a blanket that is set aside to be worn only by a chief. This is signified by the band of beadwork that runs across it in the middle.

Within the context of this liturgy, it represents the leadership of God our Great Father whom we follow and who calls us to peace and unity.

Altar Covering: Chief's Blanket

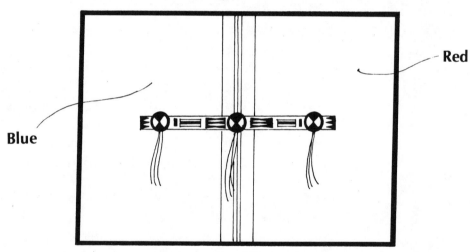

Red

Blue

Sanctuary Banners:

The two banners hang in the sanctuary stand on either side of the altar or the rear of the sanctuary.

They are larger versions of beadwork or leatherwork designs and do not stand for anything in particular, but by their colors lend an atmosphere of festivity.

Sanctuary Banners

Yellow/Gold

Orange/Yellow

White Background

Bibliography

1. **American Indian and Christian Missions,** Studies in Cultural Conflict, Henry W. Bowden, University of Chicago Press, 1981.
2. **The American Indian and the Church,** Paul Manhart SJ, Position Paper, 42nd Annual Tekakwitha Conference, Albuquerque, NM, 1981.
3. **Black Elk Speaks,** John Neihardt, Pocket Books, 1972.
4. **Christ and the Pipe,** William Stolzman, SJ, Register-Lakota Printing, Chamberlain, SD, 1986.
5. **Cultural Adaptation of the Liturgy,** Anscar J. Chupungco, Paulist Press, 1982.
6. **Dakota Theology,** Cassette and Paper, Fr. Stanislaus Maudlin OSB, Blue Cloud Abbey, Marvin, SD.
7. **Environment and Art in Catholic Worship,** Bishop's Committee on the Liturgy, NCCB, 1978.
8. **The Dialogue of Life:** The Church and the World's Religions, ORIGINS, Volume 12, #46, April 28, 1983.
9. **Finding A Way Home:** Indian and Catholic Spiritual Paths, Patrick J. Twohy SJ, University Press, Spokane, Washington, 1983.
10. **Fools Crow,** Thomas E. Mails, Avon Books, NY, 1980.
11. **The Gift of the Sacred Pipe,** Joseph Epes Brown, University of Oklahoma Press, 1982.
12. **Indian and Jesuit,** James T. Moore, Loyola University Press, 1982.
13. **Jean de Brebeuf,** Joseph P. Donnelly SJ, Loyola University Press, 1975.
14. **Lakota Ceremonial Songs:** John Around Him and Albert White Hat, Sinte Gleska College, Rosebud, SD, 1983 (book and cassette).

15. **Lakota Myth,** James Walker, University of Nebraska Press, 1983.
16. **Lakota Oral Tradition,** Tom Simms, Sinte Gleska College, Sinte Gleska College News, Summer-Fall, 1984.
17. **Lakota Ritual and Belief,** James Walker, University of Nebraska Press, 1980.
18. **Lame Deer:** Seeker of Visions, John Lame Deer and Richard Erdoes, Pocket Books, 1972.
19. **Modern Indian Psychology,** John F. Bryde, Institute of Indian Studies, University of South Dakota, 1971.
20. **Native American Catholics:** Blending Traditions, Joanne Asperheim, St. Anthonly Messenger, January, 1982.
21. **New Catholic Encyclopedia,** McGraw-Hill, 1967: "God pages," 535-562; "God the Father" pages, 562-573
22. **Position Paper** of the Native American Project of Theology in the Americas, Tekakwitha Conference, Detroit, MI, July/August, 1980.
23. **Position Paper:** With Primary Focum on Liturgy, Carl F. Starkloff SJ, Tekakwitha Conference, 1981.
24. **The Sacred Visions:** Native American Religion and Its Practice Today, Michael F. Steltenkamp, Paulist Press, 1982.
25. **The Sioux,** Royal B. Hassrick, University of Oklahoma Press, 1982.
26. **Songs and Dances of the Lakota,** Ben Black Bear, Sr., Ron Theisz, North Plains Press, SD.
27. **Speaking of Indians,** Ella Deloria, Dakota Press (no date).
28. **Spiritual Legacy of the American Indian,** Joseph Epes Brown, Crossroads Publishing Company, 1982.
29. **Statement of the U.S. Catholic Bishops on American Indians,** May 4, 1977, United States Catholic Conference, Washington, D.C.
30. **Summa Theologiae,** Thomas Aquinas, Volume 2, McGraw-Hill, 1964, "On the Existence of God."

31. **Teton Sioux Music,** Frances Densmore, Bureau of American Ethnology, Bulletin 61, 1918.
32. **Vatican Council II:** The Conciliar and Post-Conciliar Documents, Liturgical Press, Collegeville, MN, 1980.
33. **Yuwipi,** William K. Powers, University of Nebraska Press, 1982.

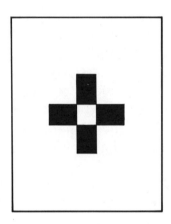

Tipi Press is an outreach of the Sacred Heart Fathers and Brothers (the SCJs), St. Joseph's Indian School, Chamberlain, SD 57325.

Ron Zeilinger has worked at St. Joseph's Indian School since 1978. He is the liturgist and Director of Religious Education at this residential school for Lakota children. He received his BA in Art Education from the University of Wisconsin-Stout, Menomonie, Wisconsin, and his Masters in Theology from Sacred Heart School of Theology, Hales Corners, Wisconsin. His other writings include: **Lakota Life, Way of the Cross, Kateri Tekakwitha** and **Black Hills** (this last in conjunction with Tom Charging Eagle). All are available through the Tipi Press.